Exploring
S O U T H E R N
NEW HAMPSHIRE

· ·

History and Nature
on Back Roads and Quiet Waters

LUCIE BRYAR

Charleston London

THE
History
PRESS

Published by The History Press
Charleston, SC 29403
www.historypress.net

Front cover image: Hunts Pond in the fall.
Courtesy of Jeffrey Newcomer, Partridgebrook Reflections.

First published 2014

Manufactured in the United States

ISBN 978.1.62619.423.6

Library of Congress CIP data applied for.

To Doug, my co-adventurer in life and on the trail.
He's taught me how to be still and take time to look at the animal tracks.

Contents

CONTENTS

Preface

$\mathcal{M}$y husband, Doug, and I started kayaking the quiet waters of southern New Hampshire in 2007 and have been paddling its smaller ponds, tidal inlets, lakes and rivers ever since. It's hard to describe the peace and relaxation we feel while on the water, gazing at a distant mountain and listening to the haunting call of a loon. Before too long, we realized that we needed some type of "nature therapy" during the colder months, too. So gradually, we added biking rail trails and snowshoeing fields and forests to our outdoor activities.

Our aim has always been to experience the simple beauty of southern New Hampshire, slow and easy. There's no speed, no competition and no adrenaline rush in what we do. We paddle, we bike, we walk, we snowshoe—all at a leisurely pace, taking time to drink in the simple pleasures of our "big backyard" from Keene to the seacoast.

Along the way, our outdoor adventures have led us to discover the unique history and culture of some of the smaller cities and towns in southern New Hampshire. We often drive by old cemeteries, historic sites and meandering stone walls—all with a story to be told.

This book covers a sampling of what we have found through the years—secluded ponds, off-the-beaten-path trails and small waterfalls, old mills, natural landmarks and working farms with long histories. You don't need to be a kayaker, snowshoer or bicyclist to find something interesting and useful here; you only need a sense of curiosity and a willingness to get out of your car to explore.

People often ask me, "How do you *find* these places?" While there are many postcard-picture towns in southern New Hampshire, other areas are dominated by big box stores, strip malls and interstates. The truth is you don't need to travel too far from the small urban and suburban areas in this part of the state to find some amazing natural spots, rich history and unique southern New Hampshire traditions.

Many of the natural areas and waterways we enjoy today are here only because of the relentless efforts of citizen conservationists who stepped up to fight development, clean up rivers or advocate for and build new trails. In these pages, I share information about places where dramatic preservation efforts have taken place.

I invite you to use this book not so much as a guide, but as a starting point for your own unique discoveries. Once you start exploring, like us, you probably won't be able to stop. I'm convinced that for each place we visit, there are a hundred more still waiting to be experienced. I have lived my entire life—almost six decades now—within the same eight-mile radius of southern New Hampshire and not a week goes by that I don't learn of some place new to visit. Whether you are a lifelong resident or a visitor passing through, this book has something for you.

Finding Your Way Around

The Granite State is notorious for poor signage, particularly when you get off the highways. We wouldn't want to let people know how to get somewhere, or even let them know when they have arrived, would we? Seriously, I'd be rich if I had a quarter for each time Doug and I have looked at each other and asked, "Is this the place?"

Often, when you are driving back roads, many of them unpaved, you won't be sure at first glance if this is the trailhead the book is referring to or if you have found the put-in for that hidden pond you are eager to explore. Our advice: don't be afraid to get out of your car and ask the first person you see or to venture a little farther on foot—before too long, you will figure it out. To eliminate some of the guesswork, we highly recommend traveling with the *DeLorme Gazetteer*. It has detailed information and, for this type of travel, is far superior to the New Hampshire state highway map. Finally, a good GPS never hurts.

Acknowledgements

A number of people stopped whatever they were doing to lend a hand with this book. Thank you to Eleanor Briggs, Brett Amy Thelen and Jeremy Wilson, all affiliated with the Harris Center for Conservation Education.

Special thanks to Eric Aldrich of The Nature Conservancy, who offered early encouragement, answered many questions and provided valuable insights and photos of the Monadnock Region.

Thank you to Marion Stoddart and Wynne Treanor-Kvenvold of the Nashua River Watershed Association. Marion took many hours to share details of her four decades of work to restore the Nashua River.

I am grateful to Celeste Barr of Beaver Brook Association; Molly Bolster, executive director of the Gundalow Company; and Franklin Pierce University professor and archaeologist Dr. Robert Goodby, who all took time to answer questions. Helen Cheng, a University of New Hampshire zoology student, shared her enthusiasm and knowledge of the American horseshoe crab in Great Bay.

Family members Claire and Jack Coey walked the Industrial Heritage Trail in Keene and shared their findings. Nancy Murphy, my longtime friend, not only created wonderful pen and ink illustrations but also encouraged and supported me every step of the way.

Thank you to good friend Judy King, who helped me to see that I needed to take this detour and offered her wise counsel and support in many other ways. She and her husband, Dennis, reported on Little Boar's Head Walk and provided several photos.

Acknowledgements

My daughters Meredith Horan and Lauren Bryar, both strong and accomplished young women, offer constant encouragement and inspire me to keep on exploring. Last but not least, this book would not have been possible without my husband, Doug. He has cooked too many meals to count and was always ready at a moment's notice to venture out to explore. I'm fortunate that he knows our state's back roads better than anyone else. After nearly forty years together, his deep appreciation for nature and love of history have rubbed off on me.

PART I

The Monadnock Region

• •

*W*hen you explore this corner of the state, you will find an abundance of rolling hills, meandering rivers, pristine ponds and, of course, the region's namesake mountain, Monadnock. The area's thirty-five small towns and Keene, its one small city, offer some of the most quietly beautiful scenery anywhere in New Hampshire. You hardly have to go in search of villages with white-steepled churches, picture-perfect town greens and interesting old graveyards. Just spend time driving the winding roads in the Monadnock Region, and they will find you.

Nowhere in southern New Hampshire have residents worked so hard for so long to preserve the land. Instead of a Walmart Supercenter, the region has a "supersanctuary," a term coined by conservationists at the Harris Center for Conservation Education to describe thirty-three thousand protected acres. There's plenty of "room to roam" here, at least by New Hampshire standards. There's no denying that ours is a compact state, ranking fifth from the bottom in land size among all states.

Still, the Monadnock Region seems to be leading the way in showing the rest of New Hampshire how to turn its small size into an asset. Unlike the White Mountain area, where you will find climbers in a hurry to reach the peaks, this region has an intimacy and gentleness all its own that invites you to slow down and "learn to be still."

There's a bonus to the land protection that has taken place here in recent decades: today, there are more bears, bobcats, moose, beavers, coyotes, otters and other wildlife than there were in the 1800s, when farmers working feverishly to clear the land destroyed their habitats. Red-tailed hawks can once again be seen in Keene, and bald eagles have returned to the Ashuelot River Valley. So pack a picnic lunch, bring your binoculars and be sure the shocks on your vehicle are ready for the sometimes rough and winding dirt roads.

1

Monadnock:
Mountain That Stands Alone

Those who climb to the peak of Monadnock have seen but little of the mountain.
I came not to look off from it, but to look at it. The view of the pinnacle itself
from the plateau below surpasses any view which you get from the summit.
—Henry David Thoreau

Mount Monadnock, the 3,165-foot mountain that gives this region its name, dominates the landscape in this quiet southwestern corner of the state for one simple reason: it appears to stand alone. If you were to "pick up and move" Monadnock to the rugged White Mountains to the north, it would get lost among the forty-eight peaks there that are at least 4,000 feet above sea level.

But here, near the state's border with Vermont to the west and Massachusetts to the south, Monadnock rises 2,000 feet above the surrounding landscape and lives up to its Abenaki Indian–inspired name, which means "mountain that stands alone." In truth, the mountain is part of a small ridge. But the other peaks, including its smaller twin, Pack Monadnock (2,290 feet) in nearby Peterborough, are not as prominent.

There are many vantage points in the region and many different ways to experience this alluring mountain that have inspired generations of poets, artists, writers and philosophers. When you explore the mountain, you are in the "company" of Henry David Thoreau and Ralph Waldo Emerson, both of whom loved the mountain, as did Rudyard Kipling, Mark Twain, John Greenleaf Whittier, H.P. Lovecraft and many others.

Thoreau hiked it four times between 1852 and 1860 and often kept a detailed nature and trip journal. During his camping trip in 1860, his journal entry says he carried over two pounds of salt beef and tongue, plus eighteen hard-boiled eggs with a notation to "omit eggs next time." He also took copious notes on the plant life, including the many berries (among them some mountain cranberries stewed for breakfast) that he and his hiking companion found here.

In 1846, Emerson wrote the long, sixteen-verse poem *Monadnoc* that added to his reputation as an American poet and helped to put the mountain on the map. His work drew many other intellectual and literary types to the mountain to vacation at the Halfway House, a three-story hotel built halfway up the western slope in 1858.

For the next one hundred years at least, Monadnock supporters mounted many grass-roots campaigns to fight off further development on the mountain. "Without their hard work," notes Craig Brandon in *Monadnock, More Than a Mountain*, "this treasure today would be clear-cut in spots and cluttered with mansions, radio antennas, a tramway and a paved roadway."

Why would a mountain be the site of so much private development interest? It turns out that the summit and other parts of the mountain were privately owned by a number of different people, some of them ancestors of Captain John Mason, who held the original 1629 land grant to the region from the king of England.

We can credit the mountain's preservation today to the tireless efforts of two men who worked for the Society for the Protection of New Hampshire Forests in the early part of the twentieth century. Philip Ayres and his assistant, Allen Chamberlain, spent thousands of hours tracking down landowners and convincing them to sign their property rights over to the society. Today, the mountain is collectively owned by the Society for the Protection of New Hampshire Forests, the Town of Jaffrey and the State of New Hampshire.

This mountain practically has its own fan club; some of those who have fallen for its charms call themselves Monadnophiles. Are you curious about what inspires so many people to love this simple mountain?

Hiking the Trails

You can hike the moderately challenging mountain from Monadnock State Park in Jaffrey in about three to four hours round trip, depending on your fitness level and your chosen trail. Or you can skip the hike and view Mount Monadnock from your boat on one of the nearby small lakes or ponds. Yet another option is to simply meditate in plain view of the mountain from the grounds of Cathedral of the Pines in Rindge.

If you decide to hike it, you will not be alone. Mount Monadnock welcomes about 125,000 visitors on its forty miles of trails each year. This statistic has led to an often-repeated claim that it is *the* single most climbed mountain in the United States and the second most climbed mountain in the world after Mount Fuji in Japan. We're told that forest rangers at the state park are so tired of being asked about this, they now respond, "It's the most climbed mountain in Jaffrey, New Hampshire."

Learning a little of the mountain's early natural history might give you a better understanding of why it attracts so many climbers. Mount Monadnock was once completely covered by a red spruce forest. Then the September gale of 1815 ripped through the area, stripping the mountain of its trees and top soil above two thousand feet. When wolves built dens in the blowdowns on the mountain, farmers looking to protect their livestock set fires to scare off the wolves. It seems that some of those fires burned out of control for weeks, destroying even more of the summit's trees and vegetation.

Today, the red spruce are finally making a comeback, but the summit still remains bare ledge above five hundred feet. As a result, on a clear day, Mount Monadnock offers visitors an expansive panoramic view of 100.0 miles in every direction. No matter how you get there—at 2.2 miles, the White Cross Trail is the shortest but steepest route to the top, or the much longer, less challenging Pumpelly Trail is 4.4 miles—once you reach the summit of Mount Monadnock, it's possible to see all six New England states.

Looking to the north, you can see majestic Mount Washington—at 6,288 feet, the highest peak in the Northeast—towering 104 miles in the distance. To the south, you will see Boston Harbor and the Prudential Center, about 60 miles away. To the west are the Green Mountains of Vermont and parts of the Berkshires. Added to this panorama are more than forty lakes and ponds and thirty-one cities and towns. Is it any wonder so many hikers make the climb each year?

2

Paddling in Jaffrey: Gilmore and Thorndike Ponds

*Y*ou can enjoy a unique perspective of Mount Monadnock from some of the small ponds in the area. If you decide to canoe or kayak Gilmore Pond in Jaffrey, you are in for a delight to your senses. Even in early spring— just after the ice recedes—you can often hear the exuberant sounds of local residents swimming in the refreshing water. You might wonder, from the warmth of your boat, how they can enjoy the fifty- to sixty-degree water. In the summer, if you look down into the crystal clear water, particularly in the shallow depths, you can see the brown trout that are stocked each year by the New Hampshire Fish and Game Department.

The pond is home to two nesting common loons each season, and if you are lucky, you might see them diving deep for long periods of time, then coming up with food for their baby chicks. Loons can stay submerged for long periods of time because, unlike most birds, their bones are solid. The haunting cries of the loon will fill you with a sense of peace and stay with you long after you leave the water. You can learn more about their distinct calls on page 19.

Bald eagles can be spotted here, too, sometimes sitting in treetops and other times snagging fish that have come near the surface to feed on bugs.

Aside from the sounds of swimmers and wildlife, Gilmore Pond is quiet. There are only about fifteen homes and cottages dotting the shoreline and a six-mile-per-hour "no wake" rule ensures that your time on the water won't be disturbed by powerboats. At 125 acres, it's on the small side, with not too many coves or inlets to explore. But paddle around the bend to the left of the boat launch for a distant view of Mount Monadnock, and your time here will all seem worthwhile.

Nearby Thorndike Pond, at 265 acres, is larger and more developed than Gilmore Pond. True, you won't feel alone because there are more cottages, homes and even a small children's camp along the shore. But the payoff for paddling this pond is an even more commanding view of Mount Monadnock. When the sun is at the right angle, you can see the mountain's reflection in the dark waters of the pond. With its hourglass shape, Thorndike Pond invites exploration of its marshy areas, deeper waters and small coves from end to end. It is also home to Whittemore Island, a 5.4-acre undeveloped island protected by The Nature Conservancy and the perfect spot to go ashore with a picnic lunch.

Common Loon: Haunting Voice of the Wilderness

You can identify the common loon (*Gavia immer*) by its distinct black-and-white checkerboard markings, daggerlike bill and piercing red eyes—this is truly a beautiful bird! Watch, too, for the loon's unique swimming style. While most birds have hollow bones, the loon's solid bones allow it to dive deep and stay submerged for long periods. The loon's body is well suited for life on the water and hardly at all for land, where it appears awkward. They generally only come ashore to mate and, for the females, to lay their eggs in the spring.

Very often, you will hear the mystical call of the loon long before you see the bird. If you're like most nature lovers, this intriguing call will stop you in your tracks, leaving you eager to hear more. According to the Loon Preservation Committee, loons have four distinct calls: a tremolo, a wail, a yodel and a hoot. The tremolo, also known as the "crazy laugh," is often heard at night when the loon wants to advertise its location or defend its territory. The wail call sounds like a wolf's howl and is used to communicate with other loons or to "talk" to its mate. The yodel, a long rising call with repetitive notes lasting up to six seconds, is given only by the male seeking to defend its territory or announce its arrival. The hoot is a one-note call that sounds like "hot." It is mostly used by family members trying to locate one another.

Since loons are territorial, you will generally only find one pair on a small pond or lake. Larger waterways can accommodate more loons, with each pair staking out its territory. Each pair only hatches one or two chicks per year, generally between mid-June and late July.

If you are paddling New Hampshire waters, please do your part to protect these beautiful birds, which are a threatened species in our state. After a lengthy ten-year battle with the state legislature, the Loon Preservation Committee finally won an important outcome in 2013, when a law was signed banning the use of lead fishing sinkers and jigs weighing less than one ounce; ingestion of these is the leading cause of death among adult loons.

You can also protect the birds by watching for warning displays during the nesting season, early May through mid-July. According to the *AMC Quietwater New Hampshire & Vermont* by naturalists John Hayes and Alex Wilson, "If you see a loon flapping its wings and making a racket during the nesting season, steer clear. When you see a nest site marked with buoys or warning signs, as is done on many lakes and ponds, keep your distance." A pair of binoculars or your camera's zoom lens is the best way to observe the birds from afar and to ensure that we will enjoy their haunting calls for years to come.

3

Jaffrey Center and the Old Burying Ground

*T*here is no need to lace up hiking boots or launch a boat to enjoy the Jaffrey area. History buffs and curious types will find plenty to keep them busy in Jaffrey Center alone. The Old Burying Ground behind the meetinghouse on Route 124 has many stories to tell. At least two renowned Jaffrey citizens (one actually a summer visitor) are buried here.

Amos Fortune, a well-educated African prince, was captured in his homeland and sold into American slavery at the age of fifteen. Amos served forty-five years as a slave in Massachusetts before saving enough money to buy his own freedom and that of his wife, Violate. As a freeman, Amos settled in Jaffrey, where he gained status as a prominent citizen. He became a member of the First Church and a founder of the Jaffrey Social Library. His tanning business, launched when he was nearly seventy, was so successful that, when he died in 1801 at the age of ninety-one, he bequeathed "a handsome present" to the church and also left monies to support Schoolhouse Number 7.

Schoolhouse Number 7 no longer exists, but you can see the Little Red Schoolhouse (once Schoolhouse Number 11) that was moved to its present site in 1960 adjacent to the Old Burying Ground. It is open to visitors on weekend afternoons during the summer and other times by arrangement. If you are further intrigued by the story of Amos Fortune, you can also drive by the house and barn he built in 1789 on a twenty-five-acre site on Tyler Brook. Standing much the same as when he built it, the property is accessible from what is now called Amos Fortune Road.

The Old Burying Ground in Jaffrey is the final resting spot for Pulitzer Prize–winning author Willa Cather and Amos Fortune, a famous slave. *Courtesy of Dennis King.*

The other prominent person found in Jaffrey's Old Burying Ground is a surprising discovery to many—it certainly was to us when we happened upon her gravestone unexpectedly. The Pulitzer Prize–winning American author Willa Cather was born in Virginia's Shenandoah Valley in 1873 but moved soon afterward with her family to Nebraska. Willa was raised in Red Cloud and attended the University of Nebraska. This prolific author produced many acclaimed works, most of them novels about frontier life on the Great Plains.

So why is she buried in Jaffrey, New Hampshire, you might ask? Turns out that Willa, who lived most of her adult life in New York City, enjoyed frequent visits to Jaffrey between 1917 and 1940. She would usually visit in the fall after the summer crowds were gone and stay for several weeks at a time at what was then the Shattuck Inn, not far from Jaffrey Center. She worked on several of her important novels here, often in a tent set up in a nearby field with views of Mount Monadnock in the distance. One fall, she came to Jaffrey planning to stay three weeks and ended up staying three months because her work on *My Ántonia* was going so well.

Before she died in 1947, Cather asked to be buried in Jaffrey Center's Old Burying Ground, even though the rest of her family was buried in Red Cloud. Now here's where the story of her burial takes a slight twist. According to *New Hampshire Curiosities* by Eric Jones, at the time of Willa Cather's death, the Old Burying Ground was full, and the town fathers were not sure if they could find a spot for her. Honored by her request, however, they made room for this prominent twentieth-century American novelist. That may explain why you will find her tombstone tucked away on the southwestern fringes of the Old Burying Grounds "in a low and lonely corner."

Not to worry, however. Cather's longtime friend and companion, Edith Lewis, is buried right beside her in a small gap between the cemetery wall and her grave.

You will find the Old Burying Ground behind a long horse shed, located behind the more prominent meetinghouse, which is up on a rise in Jaffrey Center. Look for a graveyard map on the western end of the shed.

4

Keene: From Jack-o'-Lanterns to Historic Ashuelot River Valley

The small city of Keene (population 23,460), home to Keene State College, is a picturesque stop in the Ashuelot River Valley. It claims to have "America's widest Main Street," which might very well be true. There's no way to verify this fact, since there's no central database on America's Main Streets, so far as we know. On the other hand, we *can* confirm that Keene holds nine world records for the most jack-o'-lanterns assembled in one spot at one time—it's a great source of local pride.

If you are visiting around Halloween, you might experience Keene's legendary Pumpkin Festival for yourself, now attended by as many as fifty thousand people each year. The world record–setting tradition started in 1992 with 1,628 carved and lit pumpkins on display, establishing a new category in the *Guinness Book of World Records*. The city achieved its hard-won ninth world record in 2013 with 30,581 jack-o'-lanterns, finally regaining the title they had lost to Boston in 2006.

In recent years, Keene has also enjoyed a friendly pumpkin rivalry with the tiny town of Highwood, Illinois (population 5,400), which managed to assemble as many as twenty-eight thousand pumpkins in 2013. Highwood faces a challenge from strong winds coming off Lake Michigan, making it difficult for them to keep their jack-o'-lanterns lit for the Guinness regulation of five minutes. Keene and Highwood were featured in an hour-long special, "Pumpkin Wars," that aired on HGTV in 2012. Today, Keene and Highwood refer to themselves as "sister cities."

Keene's location on the Ashuelot River made it a prominent and prosperous site for a number of mills in the nineteenth century. The river

Keene claims to have the widest Main Street in America. *Courtesy of Mickey Pullen.*

provided water power for sawmills, gristmills and tanneries. After the railroad arrived in 1848—with twice-daily trains from Boston—Keene became the industrial center for the region. In one early history, the town was called the "birthplace of woodenware." Companies in the area felled trees to make wooden machinery, carriages, sleighs and waterwheels, as well as other "must have" items of the day such as clothespins, chairs, pails, shoe pegs and tubs.

Magic Mud Leads to Prosperous Family Business

If you want to explore some of the area's industrial history on foot or by bicycle, you can choose from several rail trails and pathways that begin in Keene or intersect the downtown. The Industrial Heritage Rail Trail is a short one-mile jaunt starting from Eastern Avenue and ending on the corner of Railroad and Main Streets. Many of the buildings on the trail date to the 1800s, including that of the J.A. Wright Company, which is still in operation today, though under new ownership.

The company was founded in 1872 by John A. Wright, who began manufacturing a polish called Red Star Cleaning Powder. There is an interesting story behind Mr. Wright's discovery of this unique polish. In a short online company history, J.B. Wright explains that his great-great-grandfather John was driving a buggy on a back road near Keene in 1872 when he "spotted a cow mired in a muddy bog." When he stopped to help a neighboring farmer free the cow, Mr. Wright noticed the cow's legs and flanks growing lighter as they dried. Wiping the mud from the cow's bell, he also noticed that the bell appeared nicely polished and brighter.

While many people in the same situation might have scratched their heads and continued on with their day, John Wright was intrigued enough to have the mud analyzed. He learned that the substance was diatomaceous earth. Turns out the "magic mud," formed from the fossilized shells of microscopic aquatic algae thousands of years old, was perfect for polishing metal.

Wright immediately purchased the land in Troy and began marketing powders under the brand names "Red Star Cleaning Powder" and "Golden Seal Metal Polish." Through five generations of continuous operation, the company has developed and expanded its product line to include a number of brass and metal polishes and jewelry cleaners—though it stopped mining that first site in Troy long ago. In 2006, Weiman Products, LLC, purchased the J.A. Wright Company. J.B. Wright is the fifth generation of the Wright family to serve as company president.

Gathering Sap the Old-Fashioned Way

The Keene portion of the Cheshire Rail Trail, also starting from Eastern Avenue, is 4.6 miles long and includes some historic mill buildings before ending at Stonewall Farm. Stonewall is the only working dairy farm in the region that is open to the public. The property, which has been in continuous agricultural use for 250 years, features Belgian draft horses, four miles of mountain bike trails and a Discovery Room for kids ages three to eight.

Each spring, Stonewall Farm hosts a unique sap-gathering contest. As many as twenty groups of teamsters and their work horses come from all over New England to compete. This is maple sap gathering the old-fashioned way—there is no plastic tubing to transport the sap to large holding tanks. Instead, teams ride through hills and woods gathering sap from wooden buckets along a marked course. Judges award points based on technique, how much sap is collected and finishing time. Afterward, competitors and spectators alike can visit the on-site sugarhouse to see how maple syrup is made and sample a maple sundae.

Aside from maple season, you can visit the farm any day of the year between 4:30 to 6:30 p.m. to watch the milking of the organic certified cows. Since this is a working dairy farm and not a tourist destination, don't expect to be greeted by staff unless there is a special event in progress. Instead, look for self-guided tour cards in the kiosk in the parking lot.

History Dating to the Ice Age

The Ashuelot Rail Trail, which extends 21.2 miles from Keene to Hinsdale, follows an abandoned rail bed along the Ashuelot River. The unimproved trail can be accessed off Emerald Street in Keene. While the early part of the trail has some scenic points, there is a stretch from mile ten to mile sixteen that is an eyesore—due to power lines and sand piles—and also challenging to navigate by bicycle unless you are on a mountain bike.

Some folks choose to explore the ten-mile stretch starting in Hinsdale instead. One mile from the start of the trail off Route 63, you will come upon the Hinsdale Station, a true restoration of a Boston & Maine Railroad station. There's a Green Mountain Railroad boxcar and an old New Haven Railroad caboose. From the station, there are some very nice views of the Ashuelot Valley below.

For the next few miles, the trail runs along a ridge and has some panoramic views of the Ashuelot River. As you gaze out at the landscape, you are looking at ground that was once inhabited by Native Americans as many as ten thousand years ago—long before white settlers came here in the 1700s. In fact, the southern portion of the Ashuelot River Valley hosts twelve known Native American sites, ranging from the oldest Paleo-Indian site to a "more recent" Native American fort dating to 1663.

Arthur Whipple was a longtime resident of West Swanzey and an avocational archaeologist when he first discovered what he believed to be Indian artifacts along the banks of the Ashuelot. He contacted University of Massachusetts archaeologist Mary Lou Curran, who spent the next several years painstakingly excavating and studying the site.

Curran confirmed through carbon dating of caribou bones and other findings, that Whipple had in fact uncovered a very early Indian settlement. Up to this time, according to archaeologist David R. Starbuck, only isolated Indian sites had been discovered in New Hampshire, indicating that a number of tribes had passed through the region. The Whipple site, however, was the first documented settlement in the state dating back to the Paleo-Indian period, from 10,000 to 5,000 BC. Found here were a number of stone tools, fluted points and scrapers used to make tools.

As you look at this landscape, you have to imagine that it was very different when the Abenaki Indians first encountered it. They came in just after the glaciers had receded and the last of the mastodons and mammoths had disappeared. There were many more glacial lakes—"clear, cold, and lifeless," by one account—and much less land than what is here today. The Indians moved seasonally along the major river valleys, keeping to the high ground.

They hunted caribou and other game and fished in the Ashuelot and other rivers. Sadly, the Whipple site and others in the area were badly looted by artifact hunters in the late 1970s to early 1980s. In keeping with current state laws, the site is now unmarked.

All is not lost, however. Franklin Pierce University professor of Anthropology Dr. Robert Goodby has continued archaeological explorations in this region. "There are still digs going on in the Ashuelot Valley, when required by federal historic preservation law," says Goodby. In 2009, for example, the professor was called upon to lead an excavation at the site of a proposed middle school in Keene. Objects found here revealed that Indians were living at the Tenant Swamp Site at the end of the last ice age about eleven thousand to twelve thousand years ago.

5

Swanzey: Home to Four Covered Bridges

*G*ranite Staters seem to love their covered bridges. Is it the romantic idea of stealing a kiss under the roof of the bridge or the idea of a horse and sleigh making their way over the creaking floorboards? Early settlers built the bridges for the same reason they were first constructed in the Alpine regions of Europe: the roof protected the bridge floor and support timbers from snow buildup and harsh weather. The irony is that road agents of the day had to shovel snow *onto* the bridges so that sleigh runners could glide over them.

There are seven covered bridges in the Monadnock Region, four of them in Swanzey, just south of Keene. All of the Swanzey bridges cross the Ashuelot River and all are listed on the National Register of Historic Places. From the Keene rotary, if you take Route 10 south to Swanzey, turn left on Ash Hill Road and take another left onto Sawyer's Crossing, you will come to the Sawyer's Crossing/Cresson Covered Bridge.

The bridge was first built in 1771 for a cost of fifty-three pounds, six shillings. In 1859, when it was reconstructed, townspeople celebrated with a dance held right on the bridge. They hung paper lanterns from the rafters, brought in a four-piece orchestra and served food at midnight. Sounds like quite the party for a bridge!

Nearby is an interesting Paleo-Indian site referred to as Sawyer's Crossing. A historian working in the 1960s used bits and pieces of town histories and oral traditions to re-create a network of Indian trails crossing New Hampshire. Four of them intersect here at Sawyer's Crossing. If you take a

The Swanzey fish dam, or weir, was likely built by Abenaki Indians about 3,800 years ago. *Illustration by Nancy Murphy.*

ten-minute walk downstream from the bridge, you will come to the Swanzey fish dam, or weir, a large V-shaped formation of boulders on the bottom of the river now covered with a thick layer of silt.

While some local historians claim the dam was constructed by the first white settlers of Swanzey, professor Robert Goodby has uncovered much stronger evidence to support his belief that the dam was built by the Abenaki Indians about 3,800 years ago to catch shad, herring and alewives.

Leaving this area and continuing on Route 10, you will come to an intersection with Main Street. Take a left here to bring you, after a short distance, to the oldest original bridge in this group: the Thompson Covered Bridge. This bridge was built in 1832 at a cost of $523.27 and sadly, but not surprisingly given its age, is in need of some TLC today.

The Thompson Covered Bridge had a posted load limit of six tons up until 1990 when it was closed for a time and then reopened with a posted limit of three tons. At some point in the 1970s, school buses were allowed to cross the bridge only if they were empty. Bus drivers would stop the bus on one side, discharge the students to walk across the bridge and then pick them up on the other side. Can you imagine parents allowing this to go on today?

Continuing on Route 10 South, you will take a left onto Westport Village Road, where you can see the Slate Covered Bridge. This bridge, originally built in 1800, wins the prize for the greatest number of calamities. In 1862, William Wheelock was halfway across the bridge with his team of four oxen when the structure collapsed and they all dropped into the river. No one was hurt, but the bridge needed to be reconstructed, of course. In 1987, the Slate Bridge was repaired after suffering significant damage from a snowplow, and in 1993, it was destroyed by fire. The last rebuilding was in 2001 at a cost of $900,000.

The last covered bridge on the Swanzey tour is east of Route 32 on Carlton Road, a half mile south of Swanzey Village. Just past the center of town and the airport, look for Carlton Road on the left. Carlton Covered Bridge is about one-quarter mile straight ahead. The first bridge was built here in 1789, reconstructed in 1869 and rebuilt again in 1996. One account says that the builders (we're not sure which year) used a wagon fully loaded with hay to determine how high and wide to make the bridge opening.

Covered bridge in Ashuelot. Nearby are four more historic covered bridges in Swanzey. *Courtesy of Douglas Bryar.*

This last point raises an interesting question about the reconstruction of historic bridges. Who does the delicate work of re-creating those trusses, posts and crisscrossed braces so that they remain historically accurate? We don't know the answer for sure, but according to one source, it was town tradition to ask barn builders to rebuild the bridges since many barns share a similar truss system.

6

Harris Center in Hancock:
Room to Roam

*N*ature lovers visiting the Keene area will want to venture about fifteen miles east to the village of Hancock for a visit to the Harris Center for Conservation Education. You will find it from the center of Hancock by staying straight on Main Street past the church and post office for about two miles, then veering left at a fork on Hunts Pond Road and then finally turning left on unpaved Kings Highway.

As a child, Eleanor Briggs traveled from Lloyd Harbor, Long Island to spend summers at her grandmother's house in Hancock. Her grandmother lived in the beautiful summer home, complete with servants' quarters, that now serves as the Harris Center. "There were no children my age, so I would go out into the woods to play…I felt nurtured by the woods, the mosses, the beautiful brooks," she recalls.

Back home, Eleanor was equally drawn to her beloved landscape on the north shore of Long Island: "There were thirteen ponds and an abundance of ducks and geese. I used to walk through the woods to reach the Sound where I fished for flounder." Through the years, as she saw her treasured spots on Long Island getting paved over and sold for development, she resolved not to let it happen in the Monadnock Region.

"I woke up one morning in a sweat with images of skyscrapers around Hunts Pond," says Eleanor, referring to the small pond near her grandmother's house. The image motivated her as a young adult to talk with some like-minded friends about the idea for the center.

"With not much money, we decided to focus on education," says Eleanor, who after serving nearly two decades as board president of the Harris Center

Glacial erratics on a woodland trail at the Harris Center for Conservation Education. *Courtesy of Lucie Bryar.*

for Conservation Education, now travels worldwide as a photographer for the Wildlife Conservation Society. "My goal [in founding the Harris Center] was to coax everyone to fall in love with our beautiful part of the planet so they would all want to protect it."

Operating as a land trust for the past thirty years, the Harris Center now has a conservation interest in about twenty-one thousand acres reaching into seven towns. This land is part of what has been termed a supersanctuary, which covers a total of thirty-three thousand acres in the region. Meade Cadot, a conservationist and longtime director of the Harris Center, coined the term supersanctuary in part to encourage the preservation of larger parcels of land that would support animals like bobcats, moose and black bears that need a large "home range."

So what can visitors to the area see and do here? Aside from its many school outreach programs, the Harris Center offers a full schedule of lectures, films, workshops and outings for all ages and interests.

From the center, you can explore about thirteen miles of trails, all with free year-round access. Come here to walk, cross-country ski, snowshoe or enjoy an easy hike. On weekdays you can take a guided walk, led by a conservationist. If you prefer to head out on your own, you can follow the short Dandylyon and Boulder Trails on the east side of the property, which will take you to some amazing glacial erratics in the midst of a forest. Be aware when you reach the double yellow blazes, you will need to turn around and retrace your steps back to the center.

Hikers choosing the west side trails can climb to the peak of Mount Skatutakee (1,998 feet), which rewards you with some of the best views in the region of Mount Monadnock. The Cadot Trail starts at a gate off the dirt section of Old Dublin Road and after one easy mile over a rocky roadway, becomes a steeper half-mile hike to the peak. The Harriskat Trail offers a more gradual climb.

If you are intrigued with the idea of exploring all that the supersanctuary has to offer, you'll need to download a map (www.harriscenter.org) and plan to spend lots of time in this region. Understand that the land is not one contiguous property but rather is spread out through the entire Monadnock region.

In total, the protected properties offer sixteen walkable hills or small mountains, plus nineteen ponds, rivers and lakes—some of them are included as separate entries in this book. Finding trailheads and boat launch sites can be an adventure in itself. Today, we can thank people like Eleanor Briggs, Meade Cadot and many other conservation groups and town officials that both humans and wildlife have "room to roam" here.

7

Willard Pond and the
dePierrefeu Wildlife Sanctuary

A short distance from the Harris Center, on the north side of Route 123, is the road to Willard Pond, one of southern New Hampshire's most pristine quiet waters and a perfect spot to launch a canoe, kayak or other non–gasoline powered boat. Willard Pond is part of the dePierrefeu-Willard Pond Wildlife Sanctuary, which includes Bald Mountain and several walking trails.

The sanctuary was the vision of Elsa Tudor dePierrefeu, who lost her husband in World War I. Elsa hoped to create a wildlife sanctuary "For Peace Among All Beings," the saying now engraved on a commemorative rock at the sanctuary entrance. Today, thanks to donations of land and funds from the dePierrefeu family, the Harris Center and New Hampshire Audubon, the sanctuary encompasses 1,400 protected acres, making it the largest Audubon property in the state.

There is absolutely no development on Willard Pond, lending it a wonderful feeling of peace and tranquility. After launching your small watercraft from the sandy put-in, you might see common loons, wood ducks, hooded mergansers, bald eagles, hawks and herons. From your boat, you might also see tiny figures of hikers in the distance, scaling the rocky ledges of Bald Mountain (2,030 feet). There are a series of hikes here ranging from fifteen minutes to two and a half hours, and while the climb to the top is rocky and steep in spots, the view of the pond and surrounding mountains is worth the effort.

At 108 acres, Willard Pond is not large. But it is one of the cleanest, most serene waterways you will find in all of southern New Hampshire. A signature feature in the preserve is glacial boulders. Left behind by retreating glaciers centuries ago, these big rocks dot the shore and the bottom of the pond, with some jutting high above the surface. When you paddle Willard Pond, you might feel that your boat will "strike a boulder." In reality, the glacial erratics lie far enough below the surface to keep you safe. Enjoy the view and the experience.

8

Cathedral of the Pines in Rindge: Place of Beauty and Peace

$\mathscr{A}$s you make your way eastward across the Monadnock Region, you should make time to visit Cathedral of the Pines in Rindge. This is a beautiful outdoor place of interfaith worship with a stone altar dedicated to all servicemen and women who have given their lives for our country.

Altar of the Nation is set on a hilltop overlooking Mount Monadnock—offering one more view of the region's signature landmark. Cathedral of the Pines can be appreciated on a simple level: come here for reflection, inspiration and a sense of peace; look at the gardens and the stone altar and enjoy a picnic lunch under the canopied picnic area. You can also visit with a fuller understanding of its history and significance.

The fifty-five-foot tall stone bell tower that sits near the entrance is a monument to all women who have made wartime contributions, whether on the battlefield or at home. The large bronze plaques in the archways were designed by Norman Rockwell and created by his son, Peter.

If there's no one around, you can run your hands over the stones making up Altar of the Nation. The stones are all gifts from historic places and famous people from around the world. Stones have come from the homes and grave sites of U.S. presidents George Washington, Andrew Jackson, Franklin Roosevelt, Harry Truman, Lyndon Johnson and Ronald Reagan. Numerous stones came from the battlefields of World War I and World War II in Europe. One of the more recent stones, donated by President George W. Bush, came from the Pentagon following the September 11 attack on America.

The granite fountain at Cathedral of the Pines is dedicated to nurses who lost their lives in war. *Courtesy of Douglas Bryar.*

According to the Cathedral's website, in the fall of 1937, Sibyl and Douglas Sloane III of Port Chester, New York purchased the land in Rindge as a summer property. They invited each of their four children to select a corner of the 128-acre property to build his or her own house.

In 1938, before any homes were built, a hurricane ripped through the region, bringing down many trees. It was months before the Sloanes were able to assess the damage. When they finally did, according to an account in *Hidden History of New Hampshire*, "they climbed through pine needles eighteen inches deep and climbed atop a 'stepladder' of four huge, fallen pines" to discover a stunning panoramic view of Grand Monadnock Mountain. At that moment, the Sloanes made the decision to share the site with others as an outdoor chapel.

Sadly, the Sloanes' son Sandy lost his life when his B-17 bomber was shot down over Germany in 1944. When his parents, Sybil and Douglas, held a memorial service at the clearing overlooking Mount Monadnock, many townspeople turned out in support—thus began Cathedral of the Pines.

There's a final touching footnote to the story. In 1969, the mayor of Koblenz, Germany—the town where Sandy's plane was shot down—made a special trip to the cathedral and presented the Sloanes with a stone from the six-hundred-year-old bridge over the Moselle River. The special dedication service held on October 14, 1969, "symbolized the Cathedral's ideals of friendship, peace, and brotherhood."

9

Walk to Pack Monadnock on Cranberry Meadow Pond Trail

The Cranberry Meadow Pond Trail, opened in 2010, is a relatively new addition to the Monadnock Region. It takes you from downtown Peterborough to the base of Pack Monadnock, a distance of about 4.5 miles. Part of the attraction of the trail is the variety of the route. You can start by enjoying breakfast in Peterborough's quaint downtown in the morning and then walk through open fields into hemlock forests, along a winding brook to the pond. Then it's a short climb to the top of Oak Hill. From there, you will head east to the Raymond Trail taking you to the base of Pack Monadnock. If you still have energy left, you can hike another 1.6 miles to the top of the mountain.

We can hike the Cranberry Meadow Pond Trail today in large part because of one person's vision and what you might call serendipity. Swift Corwin is a private consulting forester from Peterborough. His idea to create this trail was stalled for several years—in part because he was busy with other work and in part because he wasn't sure how to address the sizable wetlands on the property.

Then Corwin traveled abroad, where he hiked from the village of Schio in Italy to the top of Mount Novegno, an experience that renewed his enthusiasm. "I knew it could happen in Peterborough," he says.

Here's where serendipity comes in. Just a few weeks after returning from Italy, Corwin learned that two landowners with large parcels were interested in building a trail along the same route he had envisioned. These landowners, along with several other private property owners,

A hiker on the Cranberry Meadow Pond Trail near Peterborough. *Courtesy of Eric Aldrich/TNC.*

eventually granted easements to the Monadnock Conservancy, which now maintains the property.

When you walk the Cranberry Meadow Pond Trail, remember to stay on the trail since you are on private land. If you start from Cheney Avenue in downtown Peterborough, you will cross Old Street Road and then cross a swamp—with dry feet, thanks to a boardwalk built by a dedicated group of volunteers.

From there, the trail parallels and then crosses a brook. "The walk along the brook is really special because it's always changing, depending on the seasons," says Corwin.

Cranberry Meadow Pond, about one and a half miles from the trailhead in downtown, was named by a struggling farmer who once planted cranberries here. Continuing on, the trail takes you through a working forest to the base of the mountain.

You can approach this trail from either end—starting from Cheney Avenue in Peterborough or at the opposite end from East Mountain Road inside Miller State Park. Some hikers choose to park in Depot Square in downtown Peterborough and walk up Pine Street to Cheney Avenue, a distance of about one mile before reaching the trailhead. As an alternative to doing the nine-mile round trip, you could also leave a vehicle at both ends.

10

Grass-Roots Effort Saves Sheldrick Forest

It has the feel of a sacred place.
—Peterborough forester Swift Corwin,
referring to a five-acre stand of old trees he helped to preserve

*H*ere in New Hampshire, we don't have anything approaching the beauty and splendor of the centuries-old cathedrals of Europe. But for true nature lovers, Sheldrick Forest Preserve is a chance to step back in time and discover "cathedral-like stands of 150-foot high white pines, hemlocks and oaks," according to The Nature Conservancy, which now owns the property. A 5-acre portion of this 227-acre property offers a rare glimpse into New Hampshire's landscape as it was when early settlers lived here. While most of our forests had been cleared for timber or pasture by the mid-1800s, you might say "they forgot a spot" in this corner of West Wilton.

There's a remarkable story of grass-roots conservation and the power of one individual to make a difference behind the creation of Sheldrick Forest. For nearly one hundred years, the Sheldrick family, who owned the property, left large sections of the forest undisturbed. But when the last family member passed away in 1994, their estate lawyer sold the property to a developer who had plans to harvest its timber, mine its gravel and build a housing development.

Enter Swift Corwin, the same forester responsible for the Cranberry Meadow Pond Trail. Corwin had been hired by the developer to tag trees over twelve inches in diameter that would be valuable to sell for lumber.

Relating the story today, Corwin says that bids had already been put out to lumber companies when he realized he had stumbled on "something really special here." What he had discovered in Sheldrick Forest was that rare five-acre stand of large, mature hemlocks and pines, some as old as two hundred years old. He points out there are also some interesting geological features on the property, including several eskers and big kettle holes left from the last ice age.

Based on his findings, Corwin convinced the developer to let him pursue another buyer for the property—one who would protect the land from logging and development. He contacted officials from the New Hampshire chapter of The Nature Conservancy, who agreed the land was worth saving and immediately launched a robust campaign to "Save Sheldrick Forest." The developer had settled on a price tag of $550,000, but gave the conservancy only thirty days to raise the money!

The "Save Sheldrick Forest" drive became a widespread regional effort, fueled in part by some spirited neighbors of the Sheldricks. Randi Stein and Judi Cahoon, two of those neighbors, made significant donations to the campaign. Townspeople throughout the area held bake sales, poetry readings, raffles and concerts to help save the forest. Students at the Pinehill Waldorf School paid a quarter each for a "dress-down day."

"Nickels and dimes bought that forest," Judi recalled in a newspaper article marking the fifteenth anniversary of the preserve. At last, after the developer granted an eleven-month extension for the purchase, Sheldrick Forest became the protected property of The Nature Conservancy in 1996.

Today, there are over three miles of trails through the forest. These trails connect with an additional eight miles of trails to the south on the Heald Tract (owned jointly by a private landowner and the Society for the Protection of New Hampshire Forests) and an additional two miles of trails to Pratt Pond in Mason.

"It's a remarkable place, especially for this growing part of southern New Hampshire," says Eric Aldrich of The Nature Conservancy. "You get into Sheldrick's woods and you lose the roar of traffic. I've heard barred owls here. I've seen deer and signs of eastern coyotes and fisher here. It probably holds bobcats. It's a great place to get away and discover a little bit of the wild."

While you are in Sheldrick Forest, be sure to explore the Laurel Ridge Trail. According to The Nature Conservancy website, the trail "climbs an esker ridge which overlooks Morgan Brook and a steep ravine, making it a great place to observe the beauty of the forest."

An esker ridge, formed by glacial streams, can be found in Sheldrick Forest in Wilton. *Illustration by Nancy Murphy.*

When you visit, park your car in a field off Town Farm Road. After crossing the field, you can take Helen's Path on the right, which drops into the valley of large trees along Morgan's Brook. Corwin says, "To the untrained eye, they just look like trees, not too different from other trees." But pause a moment to look at their girth and their height—some are thirty inches in diameter and as tall as 150 feet high and you may begin to share the sense of wonder that first led to the creation of Sheldrick Forest.

11

Pickity Place, Uncle Sam's House and Maple Sugaring

$\mathcal{M}$ost people come to Mason to enjoy a five-course gourmet lunch at Pickity Place, if they can find the place. This charming little red cottage, built in 1786, is located in the woods at the end of a winding dirt road. You will find it by taking Route 101 West or East all the way to Route 31 South. Travel five miles to the blinking yellow light in Greenville and then turn left on Adams Hill Road. From there, follow the small Pickity Place signs about two miles to Nutting Hill Road.

If you think you don't need a reservation for a place that is so hard to find, you would be mistaken. This small cottage has a tiny dining room that fills quickly, so call ahead. The gourmet menu changes month to month and features fresh herbs from the on-site garden.

In 1948, when Golden Books asked Caldecott Medal–winner Elizabeth Orton Jones to illustrate the tale of Little Red Riding Hood, this cottage was her inspiration. The folks who operate Pickity Place have fun with its history, setting aside a small room where the "wolf" hangs out in Grandmother's bed.

Uncle Sam Lived Here?

Another local house that has had a "brush with fame" is Uncle Sam's House on Valley Road in Mason. Uncle Sam's house? Isn't he a fictitious icon?

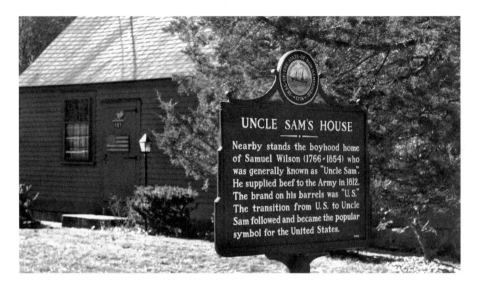

Sam Wilson, the inspiration for Uncle Sam, grew up in this house in Mason. *Courtesy of Douglas Bryar.*

Well, yes and no. A real-life Samuel Wilson (1766–1854) grew up in Mason in a red clapboard house on four acres.

At the young age of fifteen, Samuel joined the Revolutionary army, where one of his duties included slaughtering cattle and packaging meat for the troops. When he left active service, he and his brother settled in Troy, New York, near the Hudson River. They established a successful business supplying meat to the army during the War of 1812. It seems that Sam was a popular guy who was affectionately called "Uncle Sam." When he stamped his barrels "U.S." for the United States, some folks quickly associated the initials with "Uncle Sam."

How the transition came about from "Uncle Sam," the meatpacker and successful businessman, to the popular figure we know today is unclear. We do know that the house Samuel Wilson lived in in Mason was historically restored in 1966, about the same time that the State of New Hampshire placed a historical marker here. There's a private mini-museum on site that is open by appointment only.

Maple Sugaring in Lyndeborough

Have you ever visited a sugarhouse during maple season? Ever peered into a wood-fired evaporator filled with boiling sap? How about sampled hot dogs boiled in sap? Welcome to maple sugar season in New Hampshire.

In March and April, when the sap is running, most sugarhouses in the state welcome guests for tours and sweet treats. Some maple houses welcome visitors year round, not just during peak production times. A word of caution: If you set out to explore sugar shacks in southern New Hampshire while the sap is running, be prepared for muddy back roads.

The Maple Guys, owned by Chris Pfeil, recently built a new sugarhouse on Cram Hill Road in Lyndeborough. The drive out there, on a gently ascending road, has some classic New England views. When you arrive, it's easy to think that not too much can be going in such a small, unassuming wooden building in the "middle of nowhere." But once you step inside, you are reminded that first impressions can be deceiving.

Pfeil runs a full-scale operation dedicated to helping other small maple producers. He is a major supplier of evaporators and other equipment to the industry and also has a couple of inventions to his credit, including something called an Acc-u-cup and another called the Hands-Free Bottling System. The award-winning maple producer is currently at work on a new filter press.

It's safe to say that New Hampshire producers will never catch up with the much larger Vermont operators, who produce 40 percent of the nation's maple syrup, or with their Canadian neighbors to the north, who produce 75 percent of the world's supply. No matter. If you take time to visit some of the smaller maple sugarhouses in the Monadnock Region—there are about twenty of them listed on the New Hampshire Maple producers website—you should come away with a "sweet" appreciation for this labor-intensive and weather-dependent industry.

Under the best conditions, a sugar maple tree reaches tapping size in about thirty to forty years, after which a healthy tree can continue to produce sap for sixty to seventy years. It takes about forty gallons of sap to produce one gallon of maple syrup, yet each tree only produces about ten to fourteen gallons of sap in an entire season. If you do the math, you can see that it takes a lot of trees to run a profitable maple business. The Maple Guys, like other small producers, lease some trees from the Society for the Protection of New Hampshire Forests.

Maple producers like Chris Pfeil grade their syrup based on strict guidelines set by the industry: Grade A–light amber has a delicate flavor and is produced from the first few runs of sap. Grade A–medium amber has a richer maple flavor and a little deeper color, and Grade A–dark amber has a stronger, more robust flavor. Grade B has the darkest color and flavor and is usually used in cooking.

You don't need a recipe to enjoy a uniquely New England tradition. "Sugar on snow" is made from clean snow with maple syrup poured on top. Some sugar shacks charge you for a serving and even offer a cider donut, saltines or sour pickles to go with it. You can certainly make your own sugar on snow—sometimes called "leather aprons" — if you understand that you first need to boil the syrup to the soft candy stage (225 degrees on a candy thermometer) before drizzling it on the snow. The result is a sweet and chewy taffy—very reminiscent of a scene in Laura Ingalls Wilder's *Little House in the Big Woods*.

12

Purgatory Brook Falls:
Party at the Pavilion, 1800s Style

*P*urgatory Brook Falls is a quiet little gem in what seems like an unlikely spot. The 550-acre property, with three small waterfall features, straddles the towns of Mont Vernon and Lyndeborough. It has a secluded feel even though it's only about one mile off busy Route 101. When you come to explore this area, you should expect to find mud in almost all seasons.

You can hike from the lower falls all the way to the upper falls, a distance of about three miles, over terrain that includes tree stumps, boulders and slippery muddy areas. Or you can hike from the lower falls to the middle falls before returning to your car to drive to the upper portion.

To drive to the upper falls, turn right from the small parking area onto Center Road and continue to the end of Purgatory Falls Road. From there, walk about one mile on Upton Road until you reach the upper falls.

Purgatory Brook Falls is a compact property, not an expansive site. The parking area and first few hundred feet of the lower falls trail are littered, making a poor first impression. But as you continue on, the landscape gets cleaner and more inviting. The path is shady and cool, and before too long you will reach the lower falls, where the brook cascades down about thirty feet through the rocks.

Starting in 1811, Purgatory Brook Falls supplied water power for a number of successive lumber mills until the mill buildings were destroyed by fire in the 1950s. At the time, the mill was owned and operated by William

Falconer, a well-known Milford surveyor. In 2008, a Falconer descendant sold the property to the Souhegan Valley Land Trust, providing access to the lower falls, the old mill site and the three-mile trail.

The upper falls have an interesting history of their own. Various town records contradict one another on some points, but they all agree that the land at the top of the falls was the site of entertainment in the late 1800s. One history says a grand hotel here once drew vacationers from as "far away as Boston," while another source says there was a pavilion, games and picnic area.

The parties held at the upper falls attracted anywhere from three hundred to two thousand people. Today, the only visible reminders of this "party spot" are iron posts in the rocks. They once supported a viewing platform over the falls for visitors. Can you imagine all those "tipsy" partyers peering down into the falls?

Near the top of the falls there's a naturally deep hole in the rock, sometimes called the Devil's Bean Pot. If you climb down into the hole, you will reportedly find names and dates carved into the rock dating back to the 1800s. In a booklet of *Hikes in the Piscataquog Region*, author Ian Tucker Peach explains, "It is legend that the Devil would lure the townspeople into the Purgatory Falls forest by promising to cook them a baked bean supper in this large bowl shape in the rock."

While Purgatory Brook Falls is not a large property like the well-known Flumes in the White Mountains, it is a nice little discovery not far off the main road. The Purgatory Brook watershed connects to the north with the Pisquataquog River and to the south with the Souhegan River, providing habitat for heron, foxes, deer, moose and other wildlife.

PART II

The Merrimack Valley

• •

*T*o many visitors, the Merrimack Valley is a traffic-clogged artery on the way to the mountains or the lakes region. We can probably blame the Merrimack River for the fact that this part of southern New Hampshire is not a tourist destination. The river and its tributaries once powered many industries, including the world's largest cotton mill, built in Manchester in the 1800s. Large numbers of immigrants from Canada and other countries were attracted to the region to work in the mills. They first came for jobs and then settled here permanently; today, more than half of the state's population, an estimated 628,000 people, call the Merrimack Valley home.

There is a rich cultural and industrial history in the region, but where are the pristine ponds, picturesque town centers and nature trails that are so much a part of the Monadnock Region? If we start by looking for something different, we won't be disappointed.

You could call this region "the comeback kid." Nashua, the state's second-largest city, is filled with shopping malls, six-lane roads and tightly developed neighborhoods. The Nashua River, however, once named one of the top-ten dirtiest in the country, today is home to abundant wildlife and a favorite site for kayakers and canoeists. The Nashua River Rail Trail, stretching from Nashua to Ayer, Massachusetts, is well-loved and used by bikers, walkers and in-line skaters.

Anadromous fish—those born in fresh water but live out their adult lives in the ocean—were once barred from making their journey by dams built on the Merrimack River. Today, a unique public/private partnership at the

Amoskeag Fishways allows Atlantic salmon, sea lamprey, shad and herring to make the trip up a series of ladders.

In the same vein, the bucolic Robert Frost Farm in Derry, sold by the family in 1911, was left as a car junkyard for many years before finally being restored to its original beauty in the 1970s.

Finally, if you are willing to get off busy Route 101A, which runs east to west across the southern part of this region, you will find some interesting back roads and natural sites through Amherst, Bedford, Hollis, Mont Vernon and New Boston. Likewise, if you venture off the north–south corridor of Routes 293 and 93, into the towns of Boscawen, Bow, Canterbury, Deerfield and Henniker, to name a few, there are still natural and historical treasures to be discovered.

13

Merrimack River: Powerhouse for the Mills

Merrusquamack, Merimacke, Merimack, Merrimacke,
Merrimake, Merrymake, Menomack
[Various early spellings for the Merrimack River]

The Merrimack River begins in Franklin, New Hampshire, and runs south through the region for about sixty miles before flowing into northeastern Massachusetts. There it takes a northeast turn in Lowell before emptying into the Atlantic Ocean at Newburyport. Thousands of years before European settlers first arrived on the Merrimack in 1605, this "place of strong currents" was a renowned spring fishery for Native Americans, home to an abundance of salmon, shad, lampreys, herring, eels and alewives.

Nowhere in southern New Hampshire does the history and wild power of the Merrimack River meet more dramatically than at a fifty-four-foot drop in the river called the Amoskeag Falls, near the Manchester mill buildings. There's a historical marker here, accessible from a parking lot off North Commercial Street, which reads in part: "The falls at Amoskeag (a 'place of many fish' in the Algonquian language) has been popular for at least eleven thousand years as a place to meet, fish, and listen to the river. The great Pennacook leader Passaconaway and his son Wonalancet spent much time here."

With the help of a historical article by D. Benner in *Merrimack Valley Magazine*, we can picture what it may have looked like as Native Americans fished here each spring: "Using long-handled dip-nets, [they] would scoop

A historic marker overlooks Amoskeag Falls, once a thriving fishery for Native Americans. *Courtesy of Lucie Bryar.*

fish out of the water as they tried to climb waterfalls. Clubs, spears and even bows and arrows were used to dispatch exhausted fish sitting in the shallows or trapped in the weirs. Larger nets, made from the woven fibers of spruce and elm and weighted with rocks to hold them on the bottom, were dragged through the deeper pools. Along the banks, women, children and elders, using stone bladed knives, cleaned and filleted the catch."

Native American Discovery on the River Bank

We know much of what we do today about early Native American life on the Merrimack in Manchester because of an amateur archaeologist and volunteer named Peter McLane. In 1967, the State of New Hampshire planned to expand the Amoskeag Bridge on what was then the Smyth property. Before construction began, members of the New Hampshire Archaeological Society were given permission to excavate the site, which they believed would hold some important artifacts. In the summer of 1967, McLane joined a group of volunteers who dug on the east bank of the river, just north of the Amoskeag Falls.

The group uncovered some important findings, many of them dating to a time about five hundred years ago when Indians and Europeans first made contact on the riverbanks—a time that archaeologists refer to as the "Contact Period." But McLane became convinced that the nearby Neville site would hold even more significant history, and he was right.

After receiving permission from the state, he worked tirelessly through the spring and summer of 1968—sometimes alone and sometimes with his three sons—to dig test pits five feet square and six feet deep at the Neville site. What they discovered in the bottom three feet of the pits was the most remarkable archaeological find in the Northeast to date: they dug up Native American tools that were carbon dated to between 7,000 to 7,800 years old—much older than those found on the Smyth site.

Most notable among their findings was the Neville point, a projectile with a symmetrical body and carefully shaped tip used for piercing. This finding confirmed that many thousands of years ago, Native Americans in New

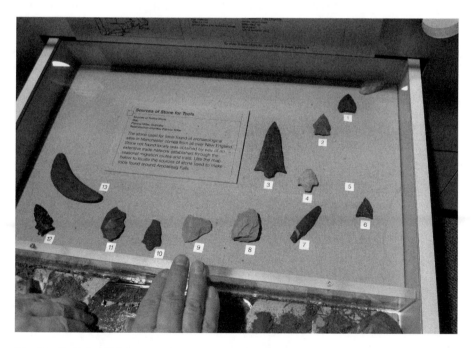

The Neville Point (#3), a symmetrical arrowhead, linked Indians in our area with others along the Atlantic coast. *Courtesy of Lucie Bryar.*

Hampshire had cultural links to other Indian societies along the Atlantic coast, from Maine to Staten Island, New York.

You can't visit the Neville, Smyth or other nearby archaeological sites today. Though rich with early Indian history, they were destroyed once the bridge expansion and other development took place. It's more interesting in any case, to take a look at some of the artifacts recovered here. You can do that at the Manchester Historic Association's Millyard Museum and in Harvard University's Peabody Museum, which both have Neville points and other recovered objects on display.

A Mile of Mills and a New City along the Merrimack

Without the Merrimack River and its fifty-four-foot falls, Manchester might not have grown into the state's largest city today. Early entrepreneurs were drawn to this location because they knew they could use the water power of the Merrimack to run their businesses.

If you visit the Manchester Millyard today, you might picture investors for the future Amoskeag Manufacturing Company standing on the banks of the river in the 1800s looking east to the city. With blueprints in hand, maybe these investors are talking about the skilled labor they will draw from the area. But this picture is backwards. When the Amoskeag industrialists first came here, Manchester was a small wooded village of only 125 residents, most of them farmers.

Manchester did not even remotely resemble a city in 1838, when construction of the world's largest cotton mill complex began. First came the mills; *then* came the city. Who would have guessed that in just ten years' time the area would become home to ten thousand people—all because of the Amoskeag Manufacturing Company? The mill owners brought people here from Canada, Ireland, Germany, Scotland, Greece and other countries to work for them.

They built not only a mile of brick mills but also row houses, fire houses, schools, parks and hospitals, all to serve the needs of the immigrants. But we shouldn't romanticize what the mill owners did; they were not motivated by a desire to take care of their workers but rather a desire to make a profit. It's well known that many mill owners hired young women and children—some as young as ten years old—to work long hours for little pay, often under hazardous and miserable conditions.

For true history lovers and those of us whose grandparents or great-grandparents earned a living here, the story of the rise and fall of the Amoskeag Manufacturing Company is an interesting one. Much more can be learned from some of the excellent published histories on the company and the city of Manchester.

Today, you can explore the renovated Manchester mills and the Merrimack River by taking a short stroll along the riverwalk, which is part of the state's Heritage Trail. The brick walkway begins near Arms Park on Arms Street and continues just under a half mile to the Waumbec Mills. The entire district is listed on the National Register of Historic Places.

Some visitors prefer to take a longer self-guided route suggested by the Manchester Chamber of Commerce, which starts on Elm Street. This route approaches the mills from the Commercial Street (the front side) of the complex and includes a stop in Mill 3 to visit the Millyard Museum. It also takes you past rows of connected brick houses, once home to the mill's founders and managers.

No matter which route you take, think of the rise of the Amoskeag Manufacturing Company as a series of stops and starts. It began when Benjamin Prichard first built a small cotton mill here in 1804. Prichard faced growing imports from Europe after the War of 1812 and came close to economic ruin because of his outdated equipment and lack of capital to modernize.

During the same era, Samuel Blodget of Goffstown worked for more than a decade to raise money to build a barge canal near the falls. When completed in 1807, the canal successfully opened trade between Concord and Boston—even if it did take five days to make the trip. Blodget, who had been inspired by a trip to Manchester, England, proclaimed that this spot on the banks of the Merrimack would become the Manchester of America. He was right, but it didn't happen for at least another thirty years.

Other entrepreneurs came and went—they either had vision but lacked money or had money but no managerial skills. Finally, a new group of investors entered the picture in 1831. They were Boston Brahmins with "deep pockets," manufacturing experience and names like Amory, Appleton, Lowell and Lawrence. This group played a dominant role in the growth of the Amoskeag Manufacturing Company and the history of Manchester for the next one hundred years.

At its peak between 1910 and 1920, the Amoskeag Manufacturing Company employed as many as seventeen thousand people in seventy-four textile departments. They were turning out fabric at a staggering rate of

Looms and many other historic items from the Amoskeag Manufacturing Company are on display at the Millyard Museum. *Courtesy of Lucie Bryar.*

fifty miles of cloth per hour. Over time, Amoskeag Manufacturing became famous for its ticking, sheeting, gingham and the denim it produced for Levi Strauss jeans. Earlier in its history, when the Civil War made cotton from the South scarce, the company turned to producing textile equipment, steam locomotives, steam fire engines, sewing machines and firearms.

The world's largest textile company hit troubled times in the 1920s and 1930s, however. It struggled to meet the challenges of worker strikes, the Great Depression and a switch from water power to new energy sources. The Amoskeag Manufacturing Company abruptly closed its doors on Christmas Eve 1935. Plans to reorganize were dashed the following year when a massive flood hit the area and the overflowing Merrimack River damaged many of the mills that it had once powered.

What you see as you walk here today is a shadow of the mills' former life. In its prime, the massive "mile of mills" was enclosed by iron gates and fences—there were large brick buildings on both the west and east banks of the river and two canals between, with footbridges connecting both sides.

And don't forget the railroad tracks running through that brought cotton from the South. In the 1960s and '70s, the two canals were filled in, and half of the buildings were torn down to make way for parking lots and streets. Even at half its former size, the historic Amoskeag Millyard still dominates Manchester's skyline today.

The renovated mills are now home to offices, restaurants, software companies and the Millyard Museum, which is definitely worth a visit. If you are curious to see inside a renovated mill building but don't have time to visit the museum, stop in at one of the restaurants. The Water Works Café, accessible from the riverwalk, has high ceilings, light streaming through soaring windows, well-worn wood floors and warm brick walls.

As you sit and enjoy a cup of coffee, contemplate how the Merrimack River—mostly a scenic backdrop today—was once a major source of power and industry that shaped the entire region.

The Amoskeag Manufacturing Company, once the largest cotton mill in the world, occupied both banks of the Merrimack River. *Courtesy of Library of Congress.*

Exploring the Merrimack by Boat and on Foot

If you want to put a boat into the Merrimack River, you'll need to do your homework first. While the Department of Fish and Game lists sixteen official launch sites, a few are barely accessible because of overgrown vegetation. Some sites have boat ramps suitable for powerboats while other sites can only accommodate carry-in canoes or kayaks. The Merrimack also has some class I and II rapids—near Arms Park in Manchester is one spot—so if you are looking for quiet water, you will need to choose your launch site carefully. One site for both car-top and trailered boats is in Nashua behind Greeley Park, accessed from Hills Ferry Road off Concord Street.

Aside from the riverwalk in Manchester, there are a number of places to walk along the river's sixty-mile New Hampshire stretch, including some trails in Concord on the property of the Society for the Protection of New Hampshire Forests. Bear in mind that many of the trails are not all that scenic since you are looking down about fifteen to twenty feet to the river below, often through trees and, sometimes, trash left behind.

If you venture out on the river or the trails, be on the lookout for bald eagles, a once endangered species that has been restored on the banks of the Merrimack. The latest census showed up to twelve bald eagles spending winter on the river in Manchester. Only eagles older than five years old have the characteristic white head and tail. Regardless of their age, however, they all have a wingspan in excess of six feet.

14

Lake Massabesic:
Outdoor Playground Near the City

*I*f you live in the Manchester area, you are probably well acquainted with Lake Massabesic, which straddles the city of Manchester and the town of Auburn. The lake is made up of two irregularly shaped bodies of water connected by a narrow channel, with the sections sometimes referred to as Front Pond and Back Pond. For more than 130 years, Massabesic has served as the water supply for Manchester and parts of six surrounding towns.

Most locals have already discovered this natural treasure; they and their parents and grandparents before them have been "playing outdoors" here for more than 150 years—though we'll see in a minute how dramatically that play has changed with each generation.

Visitors from outside the area are apt to overlook Massabesic, dismissing it simply as a large reservoir visible from the Route 28 Bypass. Not so fast! Even though swimming is strictly prohibited in the lake, Massabesic and its eight-thousand-acre watershed are well worth exploring in all seasons. You can come here in the warmer months to sail, fish, canoe, kayak, put in a small powerboat or just enjoy the wildlife. Ice fishing and skating are popular in winter.

Aside from water sports, the on-site Audubon Center offers a wildlife sanctuary and more than five miles of shoreline trails. Also directly adjacent to the lake is a trailhead for the Rockingham Recreational Rail Trail, one of the state's longest multi-use trails. All of this is easily accessible, just minutes from downtown Manchester.

"Little Coney Island"

The Indian name *Massabesic*, meaning "the place of much water," is a fitting name since this 2,561-acre lake holds 15 billion gallons of water. More than 17 million gallons are delivered each day to people in the Greater Manchester area. It may seem large for southern New Hampshire, but Massabesic is only about one-twentieth the size of Winnepesaukee, the state's largest lake.

Lake Winnepesaukee draws far most tourists today, but in the mid-1800s, Lake Massabesic held that distinction. The lake was once a booming summer resort area, well known throughout New England. Each summer, thousands of local mill owners and workers, as well as wealthy Bostonians, were attracted here for fun and relaxation. It even earned the nickname of "Little Coney Island."

Lake Massabesic reminds us that the history of a place is all about a moment in time. In one or two generations, the entire landscape and feel of a place can change dramatically, leaving behind only fading memories. Once those memories die, we are left with references in local history books and old newspaper clippings.

If you come to the narrow shores of Lake Massabesic in summer today, you'll see people sitting on blankets and in lawn chairs, watching sailboats on the sparkling water. Some are peering through binoculars at the resident loons while others are fishing from the shore or launching small boats. It's all pretty serene.

But if you had been here in 1850, you would have seen a busy shoreline dotted with boat clubs, taverns, restaurants, dance halls and grand hotels. The most famous of the hotels was the Massabesic House, an elegant Neoclassical structure with a function hall, horse stables, and a children's zoo. For a five-cent fare, an electric trolley brought people here from downtown Manchester. The city even extended its rail line to the lake and built a large train station nearby to accommodate Boston travelers.

Once here, many visitors took scenic steamboat rides up and down the lake, on any one of a half dozen steamboats operating at any given time. One boat, the 101-foot-long *Winnie L*, could hold five hundred passengers. *Winnie* even towed a large barge behind it for moonlit dancing cruises. At other times, there were scull and sailboat races and even horse and ice boat races in winter.

There was a seedy, less family-oriented side of the lake as well. People would come to some establishments on or near Massabesic to engage in cock fighting, gambling, prostitution and heavy drinking—all of this at a time when New Hampshire had temperance laws on the books.

How and why did this once popular and lively tourist area revert back to the quiet natural site we find today? Well, it happened gradually over the span of a decade or so. Beginning in the late 1800s, Manchester city officials began to realize that the pure water of Lake Massabesic could be the solution to the growing problem of contaminated wells in the city. Slowly, they began to regulate activities on the lake and then to buy up the surrounding land.

By the early 1900s, some of the grand hotels had begun to fall into troubled financial times. Those establishments that adhered to temperance laws were struggling to compete against taverns selling alcohol illegally. In a retrospective 1917 feature article titled "Fun at Massabesic," one journalist wrote, "Temperance people may wonder why the sale of ale, beer, wine and different distillery products was allowed…in a prohibitory state, but we cannot give a definite answer because we don't know of any definite answer to give." Some newspaper accounts indicate that while police routinely made arrests at the lake for public intoxication, they failed to enforce prohibition of the sale of alcohol.

Exploring by Boat

Lake Massabesic doesn't have much nightlife today—unless you count the nighttime calls of the loons or the quiet chatter of canoeists and kayakers who show up for full-moon paddles hosted by the Appalachian Mountain Club. In addition to loons, Massabesic's watershed is home to deer, raccoons, foxes and hawks, among other species. Game fish include large- and small-mouth bass, white and yellow perch and trout, sometimes stocked by the New Hampshire Fish and Game Department.

There are three public boat launches on Lake Massabesic. One is in Auburn Village just past the town hall. The second launch is off Route 121 near the Manchester-Auburn town line, and the third, designed only for canoes and kayaks, is at Deerneck Bridge on the Route 28 Bypass.

In summer, Lake Massabesic is often crowded with sailboats, particularly on the so-called Back Pond on the western side of Deerneck Bridge. The Massabesic Yacht Club, in operation since 1938, offers sailing lessons and a weekly racing program on the lake. If you are in a canoe or kayak, you'll probably want to stay on the less congested Front Pond.

Before you visit Lake Massabesic, be sure you are well acquainted with the water protection rules since they are strictly enforced by "the men and women in green uniforms with gold badges" who work for the Manchester Watershed. "No swimming" really means no part of your body can come into contact with the water. This means you cannot dip a finger or a toe in the water or allow your toddler or dog to run to the water's edge.

Boating is allowed on most sections of the lake with a limit of thirty miles per hour—while other well-marked sections are off limits. Any sport that would put a boater in contact with the water is prohibited. This includes sailboards, jet skis and most inflatable crafts. Some people are annoyed by all the rules and the enforcing officers at Lake Massabesic. Keep in mind they are not there to spoil your fun but rather to ensure that the water supply stays clean.

Nearby Walking, Biking and Snowshoeing Trails

The Massabesic Audubon Center and Wildlife Sanctuary rents snowshoes and offers a year-round schedule of nature programs. On your own, you can take a walk or snowshoe trek on the five-plus miles of Audubon trails, all of them taking you to the shores of the lake. The Wildlife Sanctuary offers the chance to see bluebirds and other grassland birds in warmer months, osprey in the spring (there's an osprey blind) and bald eagles in winter. Those on foot or snowshoes will enjoy a walk through the woods along wide trails with an open canopy—you get a mix of big trees and big sky instead of the often closed-in feel of a forest trail.

The twenty-seven-mile Rockingham Recreational Rail Trail is also accessible from the shores of Lake Massabesic. If you want to ride a flat, paved rail trail—don't come here. There's no pavement and not much smoothness on the Rockingham Trail, which runs from Manchester all the way to Newfields, near the seacoast. The surface is mostly hard-packed sand, gravel and dirt—best attempted on foot or with a hybrid or mountain bike.

In true New Hampshire fashion, this is a mixed-use trail open to horseback riding, cross-country skiing, snow mobiling and mushing. That's right, people bring sled dogs here for a workout in winter. It's always smart to know in advance who might be sharing the trail with you.

What can you expect to see on the Rockingham Rail Trail? For starters, you'll follow the shoreline and have some great views of Lake Massabesic. Starting at about the five-mile mark, you will cross under Route 101 via shallow culverts—you'll need to duck your head to get through them. Most

Massabesic Audubon Center in Manchester has trails for snowshoeing or hiking through the woods. *Courtesy of Lucie Bryar.*

of the rest of the trail is shaded and cool, with a mix of wetlands, woods, backyards and meadows. If you are riding or walking this trail in spring or summer, be sure to bring insect repellent since there are numerous ponds, bogs and streams that attract insects.

At the midpoint in Raymond, you'll come upon several restored rail cars open to the public and an 1855 one-room schoolhouse. The Raymond Historical Society is also housed here in a former railroad depot. Inside, the society has an eclectic mix of items, including a dress belonging to Annie Oakley. If you are interested in visiting the Raymond Historical Society, it's best to call ahead for its hours.

Other features on the trail include two crossings of the Lamprey River on converted railroad bridges and some small bays and coves from Epping to Newfields. When you arrive at the trail's end, you are about twelve miles from the Atlantic Ocean. Can you catch a whiff of the salty sea air?

15

Up the Ladder: Atlantic Salmon and the Amoskeag Fishways

We are all familiar with migrating birds: geese and ducks, along with about two hundred other species, fly south each winter and return north to New Hampshire in the spring. But how many of us know about migrating fish? They are called anadromous fish and, in our region, include species like Atlantic salmon, sea lampreys, American shad, alewives and river herring. Born in fresh water, these fish live most of their adult lives in the ocean but return each spring to their freshwater home to breed or spawn.

Sounds like simple biology—which it is—except when humans step in to build dams to power mills, and the fish, unable to make it to their spawning ground, eventually disappear.

Since 1989, the Amoskeag Fishways project, through a unique public and private partnership, has worked to restore anadromous fish to the Merrimack River. The Amoskeag Fishways Learning and Visitors' Center, adjacent to a hydropower station on Fletcher Street in Manchester, is a small facility that is worth a visit when you are in the area. Open year round, the center offers hands-on exhibits and a number of educational programs geared for children.

If you want to look eye to eye through an underwater viewing window at sea lampreys (they look a lot like eels!) as they make their way up a fifty-four-step fish ladder, you will need to plan your visit during spring migration from late April to mid-June. Some young visitors mistakenly think they are looking at an aquarium when they are actually looking directly into the Merrimack

Visitors can learn about migrating fish and the Merrimack River from displays at the Amoskeag Fishways Center. *Courtesy of Lucie Bryar.*

Fish travel from the Atlantic Ocean to their breeding ground in the Merrimack River with the help of computer-controlled ladders. *Courtesy of Lucie Bryar.*

River. Since the spring migration is subject to weather and other variables, be sure to call ahead.

It's interesting to note that as far back as 1835, laws had been enacted in New Hampshire and Massachusetts requiring companies to build fish ladders at the same time they built dams. Even at that time, industrialists knew they were harming the fish population. It turns out that the fish ladders built near the Amoskeag Falls in 1835 didn't work correctly and the problem wasn't addressed again for another 150 or so years.

Today, thanks to a new computer-controlled ladder, the fish are slowly making a comeback. Each step, or pool, in the ladder is one foot higher than the preceding step, and the fish are able to make their way up the river, bypassing what is now a hydroelectric dam. A small number of salmon, along with other anadromous species, is tracked here each spring. Some of them are captured in pools in Lawrence, Massachusetts, and brought to fisheries to breed.

The Amoskeag Fishways is a joint project of the Public Service Company of New Hampshire, the Audubon Society of New Hampshire, the New Hampshire Fish and Game Department and the United States Fish and Wildlife Service. This is just one of several similar projects in the state, though the private partnership with the Public Service Company in Manchester is unique. In all, the New Hampshire Fish and Game Department monitors and maintains seven fish ladders on coastal rivers, including on the Cochecho, Exeter, Lamprey and Winnacut Rivers. You can visit any of these in spring during peak migration season.

16

Monson Center: A Step Back in Time

$\mathcal{J}$f you are interested in colonial history that has not been packaged into a commercial experience, then you should find your way to Monson Center, which straddles the Milford-Hollis line. Even if you're not a history lover, you might find this site worth a trip. This quiet and peaceful outdoor spot is a great place to walk your dog, enjoy a picnic lunch or snowshoe or cross-country ski in winter.

There are no easy directions to get to Monson Center. You have to know what you're looking for and how to find it. The property is located in Milford, but you can only access it from Hollis. From Route 122 in Hollis, take a right on Hayden Road, and after a mile, take a right onto unpaved Federal Hill Road. Keep driving until the road becomes black top again and then look for a small sign for Adams Road, which is gated. Park your car in a gravel lot just past the gated road and then walk about a fifth of a mile into the woods to the Monson Center sign.

Monson Center is a step back in time—to the period from 1737 to 1770, to be exact. It was once the site of an early colonial settlement, at that time part of Massachusetts. When you visit today you'll find some of the original dirt roads, stone walls, cellar holes, a small graveyard and the tiny Gould House Museum. At the end of the dirt lane, there's a small pond that is home to many great blue herons; as many as ten heron nests have been counted here in recent years.

A dirt lane leads to Monson Center, a colonial settlement abandoned in 1770. *Courtesy of Lucie Bryar.*

Struggling Settlement Abandoned

According to one account, the original inhabitants of Monson Center couldn't agree on where to build a meetinghouse or even if they needed a town center at all. Many of the homes were spread out across the seventeen-thousand-acre settlement, mostly because the area was so rocky that farmers just kept moving farther away from the "center" in order to find good land.

Monson never had a schoolhouse or a church; early historical records show that townsfolk voted down a warrant article for a school in 1753 and rejected raising taxes to hire a preacher five times over twenty-four years. It seems the families in Monson spent their meager resources simply trying to survive off the barren land and defend themselves from attacks during the French and Indian War.

The only public structure the village had was a pound for runaway cattle. Remnants of the pound are still visible in an open wooded section today, along with six cellar holes with historical markers about the families who lived here. The Bayley house marker, for example, reads in part: "Mr. Bayley was a shoemaker by trade, and as the shoe cobbler of Monson, he used to take his kit and his tools and go from house to house doing such making and repairing as each family might want." The marker also mentions Bayley's son, Samuel, and a grandson, Joshua, who eventually went west with the Mormons. We're told that the information was taken from the pioneers' original Bibles and town records.

In an unusual move, in 1770 the citizens of Monson petitioned the general court to repeal their town charter. They cited the "very poor, Broken and Baron" land as the main reason. On July 4, 1770, the court granted their request and the land was eventually divided among Milford, Brookline, Amherst and Hollis.

Visiting Today

You can learn more about Monson's history in the Gould House Museum, which flies a period-specific British flag. You're in luck if you visit on a day when owner Russell Dickerman is on site. He's passionate about history and about the property, which he and his late wife, Geri, purchased and lovingly restored many years ago.

In 1998, when a developer planned to build twenty-eight luxury homes nearby, the Dickermans successfully convinced the Society for the Protection of New Hampshire Forests to create easements on adjacent properties so Monson Center's remote nature would remain for future generations. Thanks to their efforts, the property now covers 269 acres.

Most historic sites are roped off or protected from visitors, but this one is wide open. While it's a pleasant enough site, there's not a lot to see here apart from the cellar holes and their markers. Many people agree that Monson is special, however, for what you *won't* find here: electricity, running water and motor vehicles. This quiet natural site with an interesting history takes you away from the distractions of everyday life.

Monson Center has also earned somewhat of a reputation among ghost hunters. They come here from time to time to record strange sounds and observe unique phenomena. Is that a drumbeat in the woods? What is that flash of lights through the trees? Perhaps they've read that Monson is a "ghost town" and mistakenly believe that it is haunted by unsettled spirits.

Because no wheeled vehicles are allowed (i.e., snowmobiles), Monson Center is a great place to visit in winter. Be aware, however, that the parking lots are not plowed, which means you will likely have to park on the road when there's snow.

17

Lake Potanipo:
Site of World's Largest Icehouse

S ome places are more interesting to explore only after you learn a little of their history. Take Lake Potanipo in Brookline, for example. It looks like a town lake with a small restricted beach and not much else to recommend it. You can only swim here (from late June to late August) if you are a Brookline resident and you've paid a yearly membership fee. But this unassuming lake has an interesting history that continues to evolve today. It also offers some recreational opportunities for nonresidents during the off-season.

Let's start with the odd name, "Potanipo." We have no clear explanation why Indians originally called it Muscatanipus, which means "Great Bear Pond." We know that when white settlers came along, they cut off the first two syllables, referring to it as Tanipus. Although "Potanipo" is clearly the name that stuck, early town maps also list it as Potanipa and Potanipus.

The lake, which is one mile long and half a mile wide, encompasses 136 acres. As you stand on the small beach, you will see Camp Tevya, a Jewish camp, just to your right and across the lake on the western shore about two dozen summer homes crammed close together. Most of the remaining lakefront has been protected from further development.

What you can't see when you stand here today is what this site looked like more than one hundred years ago, when it was home to the world's largest icehouse. The thriving Fresh Pond Ice Company moved here to the shores of Lake Potanipo from Somerville, Massachusetts, in 1890. The company originally harvested ice from Fresh Pond in Cambridge until town fathers there decided to protect the pond as a public reservoir.

That action sent company executives scrambling to find a new source of clean water.

After an extensive search, they came to Lake Potanipo, a spring-fed lake with crystal-clear water. An 1892 article in the *Cambridge Tribune* described the water as "perfectly transparent and of a delicate blue tinge." There was just one problem, however. How would the company get its ice to the Cambridge area after harvesting it from the lake? Brookline had no railroad, and it would be another decade or so before automobiles and freight trucks would become part of the American landscape.

The executives of the Fresh Pond Ice Company decided to take on the New Hampshire state legislature in a fierce battle to bring rail service here—an effort that was widely supported by people in Brookline and neighboring Hollis. When the company was finally given a charter to connect to the Fitchburg line of the Boston and Maine Railroad, it immediately began laying a rail line and constructing icehouses on the eastern shore of the lake.

The company started with nine icehouses totaling over forty-four thousand square feet under one roof. Four more houses were added later, expanding the company's storage capacity to eighty thousand tons of ice. It was indeed the largest icehouse in the world under one roof.

We can only imagine the excitement this must have created in a tiny town like Brookline with a population of only about 540 people at the time. Not only did the company provide jobs—during its peak season in winter, it employed 300 workers—but it also brought the railroad, opening up passenger and freight service to Boston from this sleepy corner of the state.

Writing in *Hidden History of New Hampshire*, D. Quincy Whitney describes a typical winter day at the Fresh Pond Ice Company:

> *Work in the icehouse began at 2:00 a.m., when boys on horses scraped snow off the ice. Then men and horse teams did the "grooving and cutting" of sixteen-foot square blocks called "floats." The men guided the floats along canals in the lake to a pier where others cut the blocks into forty-four-inch blocks that were then placed on a continuous chain moving along the front of the icehouses...All the ice harvested was stored under the eaves of this vast building with sawdust and hay added for insulation. In the heat of summer, thirty to forty railroad cars left Brookline every day, each loaded with forty tons of ice.*

We know the ending to this story, of course. Eventually, modern refrigerators made their way into American homes and ice harvesting became as obsolete as VHS tapes. By the time a suspicious fire destroyed the huge Fresh Pond Ice Company in 1935, company operations had been shut down for four years. The railroad wasn't far behind—it ceased service to the area in 1936.

Master Diver with a Love of History

Meet Brookline resident Joe King, an engineer and master technical diver with a passion for shipwrecks. Joe didn't set out to uncover the untold history of the Fresh Pond Ice Company on the bottom of Lake Potanipo, but that is exactly what he did. His interest in the lake started about seven years ago, when he first heard rumors that there was a railroad track under the lake.

Joe began diving Potanipo, photographing and mapping what he thought to be interesting artifacts in the now muddy depths—the lake is no longer crystal clear. In fact, he wasn't sure at first what he was looking at. Before too long, however, this world-class diver realized he had found an underwater archaeological site close to home. He has since completed at least eighty state-permitted dives in Lake Potanipo and recovered over one hundred tools and other items from the Fresh Pond Ice Company.

His finds include saw blades, chisels and other tools, some engraved with the maker's or the user's name. After each item has been cleaned, restored and tagged, Joe turns it over to the Brookline Historical Society, which, as of 2014, is rebuilding a hand-hewn timber barn to house these and other town treasures.

"I don't get paid," Joe said in an interview with WMUR-TV's *New Hampshire Chronicle*. "I do it for the history." Up until Joe made his discoveries, most of the company's history was presumed lost in the fire.

There are a couple of interesting side notes to Joe King's story. One is that the exact location of his dives are kept secret, in keeping with state law on archaeological sites. The other is that he prefers to dive the lake in winter and has even done so when temperatures are below zero. He told the WMUR-TV interviewers who filmed one of his winter dives that there are three reasons he prefers the coldest season: "I know I won't get run over by boats in winter. The water is clearer. And snakes and snapping turtles are in hibernation."

Lake Potanipo in the Off-Season

If you don't live in Brookline, you can still explore the lake and its tributaries by boat during the off-season. If you visit in the spring, just after ice-out, and head toward a channel on the far side of the put-in, you can explore the Nissitisit River from here. Spring is the only time the water is high enough to navigate this clean, swift-moving river. At other times of the year, you will have to portage your boat over obstacles. While we wouldn't call it "quiet water," the Nissitisit is not classified as whitewater either. The challenge here is to navigate a small and narrow winding river with not much advance notice of what lies ahead for obstacles—in this case, mostly fallen trees.

You can also canoe or kayak Lake Potanipo from an easy access put-in beside Camp Tevya, outside the "residents only" season from late June to late August.

18

Beaver Brook Association: Nature in All Seasons

*J*f you are looking for a natural place that invites quiet contemplation, then you'll want to explore Beaver Brook Association in Hollis. As one hiker notes, "There are no challenging peaks to scale, no spectacular waterfalls, no grand vistas." It's true. Beaver Brook trails are mostly flat—making them suitable for couch potatoes and families with young children. But there's a lot more here than easy hiking trails. There's a rich variety of trees, wildflowers, butterflies, birds and other wildlife—more variety than you'll find on many other trails in southern New Hampshire. Even if you can't identify different species and cultivars, you'll appreciate all there is to look at and enjoy at Beaver Brook.

Like the Harris Center in the Monadnock Region, the Beaver Brook Association combines land stewardship with conservation education. The association has several classrooms on site, including one in an "off-the-grid" yurt that is heated and powered by solar panels. Adjacent to the Maple Hill Barn on Ridge Road are beehives and twelve cultivated gardens—some for herbs, autumn plants, shade-loving plants and fragrant flowers. Beaver Brook offers many programs and activities year round, including guided hikes with naturalists, maple tree tapping, snowshoe rentals, school field trips and a summer nature camp for kids.

Two Cousins with a Shared Love for the Land

Founded in 1964 with a donation of seventeen acres of land to the town of Hollis, Beaver Brook has grown to include more than two thousand acres in Hollis, Brookline and Milford. The association was the vision of two cousins: Jeff Smith and Hollis Nichols. You could call them the "country mouse" and the "city mouse."

Jeff was a farmer, forester, logger and horticulturalist who was born and raised in Hollis at a time when the town was much more of a rural community than it is today. His cousin Hollis, a mutual fund manager at a Boston bank, grew up in an affluent section of West Roxbury. Although the two cousins came from different backgrounds, they shared a deep appreciation and love for the outdoors and nature. Hollis had attended the Roxbury Latin School in Boston and eventually served as a member of the school's board. In that role, he envisioned an outdoor place that the school's students could visit in the summer. And so Beaver Brook Association was created.

Since its early beginnings, the association has practiced responsible woodland management. This means that trees are sometimes harvested here in order to clear the forest understory and provide food sources for smaller species. These smaller species then become food for larger animals, and so the food chain continues. Some of the two-thousand-acre Beaver Brook property also serves to protect part of the watershed for two rivers: the Nissitisit and the Souhegan.

Wildflowers and Butterflies along the Trails

There are thirty-five miles of trails at Beaver Brook Association, most of them accessible from near the Maple Hill Barn on Ridge Road in Hollis. The Burns Farm, a noncontiguous property in Milford, is accessed from Mason and Burns Roads, where there's a small parking area and kiosk. The Milford site has five miles of trails and abuts a number of hiking trails managed by other groups, including the Hitchener Town Forest. Activities in Milford are limited to hiking, snowshoeing and cross-country skiing.

All Beaver Brook trails are open year round from dawn to dusk, free of charge—though donations are gladly accepted. The trails marked with blue rectangles allow hikers, bikers and horses. The trails marked with yellow triangles are more delicate and only allow hikers, cross-country skiers and snowshoers.

There's an interesting feature that makes Beaver Brook Association a pleasure to explore, especially if you are not an educated naturalist. It seems that Boy Scouts, Girl Scouts and other budding environmentalists love this place. Several of them have published detailed guides to trees, butterflies and wildflowers at Beaver Brook. Abigail and Paige, two sixth-graders from the Green and White Mountains Girl Scout Troop, for example, created a detailed guide for the Wildflower Trail. It shows specific flowers, their locations on the trail and the butterflies attracted to each. You can download this guide and a few more from the Beaver Brook Association website (beaverbrook.org).

19

Derry: Home to Robert Frost Farm

Something there is that doesn't love a wall,
That sends the frozen-ground-swell under it
And spills the upper boulders in the sun.
—Excerpt from "Mending Wall" by Robert Frost

On route 28 in Derry, just a mile or so east of the traffic circle, you will find the Robert Frost Farm, open to the public since 1974. Frost was a college dropout and a struggling chicken farmer when he first came to live here with his family in 1900. He had published his first poem in 1894 and married his high school sweetheart, Elinor Miriam White, a year later. According to one account, the young couple moved here when they were in danger of being evicted from their apartment in Lawrence, Massachusetts, by a landlady "tired of several months of unpaid rent and appalled by the sight of chickens everywhere on her property."

How were the struggling Frosts able to afford such a beautiful homestead in Derry? It seems that when they were faced with eviction, Elinor quietly spoke with her husband's paternal grandfather, William Prescott Frost Sr., who agreed to purchase the thirty-acre farm. The elder Frost left provisions in his will for the young family to live rent free on the farm for ten years, after which they would own it outright.

Here, a mile from Derry Village, Robert Frost was nearly free of financial pressures. When he and Elinor took up residence on the property, it had an L-shaped farmhouse and attached barn (still here today), a large apple

ROBERT FROST
—1874-1963—
Some of the best-loved poems in
the English language are associated
with this small farm owned by the
poet from 1900 to 1911. Here Frost
farmed, taught at nearby Pinkerton
Academy and developed the poetic
voice which later won him the
Pulitzer Prize for poetry four
times and world fame as one of our
foremost poets.

Above: The historical
marker at Robert Frost
Farm in Derry. *Courtesy
of Douglas Bryar*.

Right: Poet Robert Frost
in later years. *Courtesy of
Library of Congress*.

orchard (now reduced to one apple tree), a small west-running brook (still filled with frogs) and, on the opposite side of the road, a large pasture (now gone).

Frost farmed the land, got to know his neighbors and dedicated himself in the early morning hours to writing poetry. Eventually, he also taught English at nearby Pinkerton Academy. While Robert and Elinor's life in Derry was hardly idyllic—they lost one young son to cholera shortly before moving here, and another infant daughter a few years after taking up residence—they both seemed to draw comfort from the land.

Frost spent countless hours studying nature, drawing inspiration for his poetry from the countryside around him: birches, apple trees, wood piles, pastures, snow-covered hills and starlit skies all found their way into his literary work. At least forty-one poems were written here or based on memories from his life in Derry. But it would take another twenty years and a cross-Atlantic move before Frost gained acceptance as a poet.

We know Robert Frost today as one of the most celebrated poets of the twentieth century, a four-time Pulitzer Prize winner and also winner in 1960 of the Congressional Medal of Honor for Poetry. While he spent just two months at Dartmouth College and two years at Harvard University, he went on to earn forty-four honorary degrees and read a poem at the inauguration of President John F. Kennedy.

Sadly, after the Frosts sold the farm in 1911 to move just outside London, their beloved property passed through several owners, who allowed it to deteriorate. When Elinor died in 1938, Robert Frost returned here to scatter her ashes near the brook, according to her wishes. But after seeing the site's state of disrepair, Frost decided he couldn't leave her there.

He passed by the farm again in the 1950s to find an "auto graveyard" with a sign out front that said, "Frost Acres." That prompted Frost to approach a close friend and ask if he could begin efforts to help restore it. The State of New Hampshire purchased the property in 1965, and eventually, Frost's eldest daughter, Lesley Frost Ballantine, worked with a governor-appointed board of trustees to restore it.

Today, you can visit the Robert Frost Farm in Derry and walk the short half-mile Hyla Brook Nature/Poetry trail around the property. It's a network of five paths that Frost originally cleared. Tours of the farmhouse are given for a small fee during the summer months and at limited days and times during the spring and fall.

The Nature Trail has twenty-three numbered sites but no explanations of what you are looking at. Your walk will be more meaningful if you download a trail guide from the website (robertfrostfarm.org) beforehand or get a guide from the farmhouse when it's open.

At Marker 15, you'll find yourself beside a disheveled stone wall in the woods built from a tumble of lichen-covered rocks. It's the very same wall that Frost repaired each spring with his neighbor Napolean Guay and the inspiration for his well-known poem "The Mending Wall."

We can be grateful today that, in the end, Robert Frost failed as a chicken farmer, gave up teaching and decided to devote himself full time to writing poetry. In his own words, he acknowledged, "Two roads diverged in a wood, and I / I took the one less traveled by / And that has made all the difference."And so it has.

Whose Walls Are These: If Stones Could Talk

A farmer ought to consider it his proper business,
as he has means and opportunity, to secure his lands by stone walls.
—Writer for the State Board of Agriculture, 1822

You don't have to travel too far off the beaten path in southern New Hampshire to encounter a historic stone wall. They are lost deep in forests, left across mountaintops and in plain sight in open meadows. Some towns, like Hancock in the Monadnock Region, have miles of well-traveled roadways lined with them.

Stone walls are a testament to the grit and hard work of our forebears. There's an untold story with each meandering wall—was this one built to keep in sheep or to make use of all the rocks that turned up while the farmer was tilling his soil? Did these two neighbors agree or disagree about who should repair the wall? Why do we have so many stone walls in New Hampshire and New England in general, while they are mostly absent from other parts of the country?

There are now steeper fines in place for those who steal historic stone walls. *Courtesy of Eric Aldrich, TNC.*

The answer to the latter question is pretty simple. Giant ice sheets traveled to our region from Canada about one million years ago, scraping against our bumpy bedrock and "pulling up" countless boulders. By the time English settlers arrived on our soil, however, the landscape was far different from what you might expect. Most of the boulders disturbed by the glaciers were now buried beneath organic mulch and rich forest soils.

As farmers in the eighteenth and nineteenth centuries cleared the forests for farmland, they thinned out the topsoil, exposing the subsoil underneath to winter's cold. "The combination of bare soil and cold climate enhanced the rate at which stones were heaved upward, out of the soil, by frost," writes University of Connecticut geology professor Robert Thorson. "For at least a generation of farmers, stones appeared at the surface like magic."

The state board of agriculture, as we saw, encouraged farmers to "build for the ages" and replace their wooden fences with stone walls. The goals were obvious: to clear the landscape, to protect fields from wandering livestock and to mark boundaries between properties.

Sadly, in the years since our farmlands were abandoned, many of New Hampshire's stone walls have been bulldozed for housing developments, stolen for other projects, or carted away and sold. In 2009, Governor John Lynch signed an amendment to a law first passed in 1791 that imposed fines for any person who dug up or carried away "stones, ore, gravel or sand from public lands." The fine at the time was capped at fifteen dollars, about fifteen days of wages for an average worker. For 218 years, the fine and the law remained essentially unchanged. The new 2009 law added the words "stones from a stone wall" to the list of protected resources and increased the fine to "treble damages, based on the cost of materials and restoration, and including attorney's fees and costs."

Granite Staters have developed an emotional attachment to their stone walls. Let's hope these natural treasures are preserved and protected for many generations to come.

20

Concord's Turkey Pond:
Site of History-Making Sawmill

*Y*ou could spend a full day exploring the trails and ponds surrounding the prestigious St. Paul's School in Concord—if you include leisurely time in a canoe or kayak on the Turkey Ponds. Some sources lump the two ponds together and call them both Turkey Pond; other sources refer to them as Great Turkey Pond and Little Turkey Pond. No matter what you call them, they are connected by a small canal passing under Route 89 and together offer a total of 339 acres of water.

Access to a launch site here is not easy. One short access road through the woods is covered with rocks jutting up through the dirt and is best navigated with a four-wheel drive vehicle. An alternative is to portage your boat for about one-quarter mile down a relatively steep embankment. No matter how you get here, Turkey Pond is worth the effort.

Once you are out on the water, you can expect to hear some road noise as you paddle under Route 89, and occasionally you might encounter the St. Paul's crew team. Otherwise, this a quiet spot with very few motorboats and only one boathouse on the shoreline. Turkey Pond is scenic and relaxing in large part because it is so lightly traveled. As you paddle, you will see several tree-covered islands and boulders, a variety of fragrant water lilies and a lively bird population, including migrating ducks and geese in the fall.

From Lumber Jacks to Lumber Jills

Turkey Pond is quiet today, but it was a busy place shortly after the area was hit by the hurricane of 1938. This category 3 storm first struck Long Island and then traveled across New England and Quebec, claiming nearly six hundred lives and destroying a third of New England forests. In total, 275 million trees came down, leaving the area's lumber industry at risk of collapse.

Enter the Northeastern Timber Salvage Administration (NTSA), a forerunner of the U.S. Forest Service. To help salvage the downed trees, the NTSA established temporary sawmills on Turkey Pond and other waterways in the state. They started by submerging the trees in ponds and lakes to protect them from insects and fire until they could be milled into lumber. According to the Audubon Society, Turkey Pond became the largest repository of trees in the state—12 million board feet of white pine were brought here.

Two temporary sawmills were erected on the shores of the pond, one privately run by the Durant family and the other operated by NTSA. All went well until World War II broke out, and then suddenly there was a shortage of men to operate the mills.

Violet Story, mother of six, catches up on her sewing during her lunch break at the Turkey Pond Sawmill. *Courtesy of Library of Congress; John Collier, photographer.*

Elizabeth Esty was among a group of women who milled lumber during World War II. *Courtesy of Library of Congress; John Collier, photographer.*

By 1942, "Rosie the Riveter" had already captured headlines, as women were flocking to fill male-dominated jobs. But the prevailing belief at the time was that women simply were not strong enough to mill lumber. That didn't deter the U.S. Forest Service.

They made some minor adjustments to the mill—adding more log rolling systems to minimize heavy lifting, for example—and then set about to actively recruit female workers. In a true case of "equal pay for equal work," the Forest Service offered women the same pay as men at other sawmills: $4.50 per day after a one-month training period—which was well above the average $1.60 starting wage for women at that time. There were some forward thinkers at the U.S. Forest service in the 1940s!

David Story was the youngest of six children growing up on a farm in nearby Hopkinton at the time. He recalled in a 2011 interview in the *Bangor*

Maine Times that his mother, Violet, was responsible for some of the most physically demanding work at the mill—rolling logs and hefting boards. He remembers his mother coming home from work and cooking a full meal for the family every night.

"I know she was always really proud that she did that," said David, referring to her work at the sawmill. Like most of the other dozen or so women who worked at the Turkey Pond Sawmill, Violet felt that she was contributing to the war effort. David said his mother also talked about a friendly rivalry with the men's sawmill across the pond. "[The women] always tried to beat the men—and the big deal was to see if they could out-saw them, which they did, a lot."

You can read more about some of the women who worked at the Turkey Pond Sawmill in the short book *They Sawed Up a Storm* by Sarah Shea Smith.

Turkey Pond Trails

While you are in the area, be sure to visit the Susan M. McLane Audubon Center and Silk Farm Wildlife Sanctuary on Silk Farm Road. Bordering St. Paul's School land, this is a beautiful seventy-two-acre property and "green" facility with a large nature-focused gift shop and modern classrooms.

From the Audubon Center, you can access three walking trails and just up the road, a short bike path. The Old Orchard Trail is a 1.0-mile walk that eventually intersects the Great Turkey Pond Trail, for a total distance of about 1.2 miles. Along the way, you will see high grass fields, old orchards and a mixed-hardwood forest. While both trails take you to the shore of Turkey Pond, you will get the best feel for the pond by spending time on the water.

According to an Audubon brochure, "over sixty species of breeding birds have been recorded at the Silk Farm Wildlife Sanctuary. They include ovenbirds, black-and-white warblers, black-capped chickadees, as well as white and red-breasted nuthatches."

In 2012, the city of Concord's Conservation Commission also dedicated a new 7.25-mile walking trail nearby. The West End Farm Trail connects three Concord Farms: Rossview Farm, Dimond Hill Farm and Carter Hill Orchard. Walkers can access the new trail after crossing under Route 89 near the entrance to the bike path, just past the Audubon Center. Since the trail has been made possible by easements across private land, no bicycles are allowed.

Mount Monadnock attracts more than 125,000 hikers to its bare-ledge summit each year. *Courtesy of Douglas Bryar.*

Gilmore Pond in Jaffrey has a pair of nesting loons and a distant mountain view. *Courtesy of Lucie Bryar.*

On a clear day, the view from the top of Mount Monadnock extends one hundred miles in all directions. *Courtesy of Tianne Strombeck.*

A threatened species in our state, common loons have unusual checkerboard markings and four distinct calls. *Courtesy of Tianne Strombeck.*

The Keene Pumpkin Festival holds nine Guinness World Records for the most lit jack-o'-lanterns at one time. *Courtesy of Mickey Pullen.*

Drivers and horses compete in an old-fashioned sap-gathering contest at Stonewall Farm each spring. *Courtesy of Jeffrey Newcomer, Partridgebrook Reflections.*

Cresson Covered Bridge is near a network of Paleo-Indian trails dating to about 3,800 years ago. *Courtesy of Mickey Pullen.*

A pumpkin feast along the back roads of Hancock. *Courtesy of Lucie Bryar.*

Hunts Pond is a small trout pond near the Harris Center for Conservation Education. *Courtesy of Tianne Strombeck.*

Opposite, top: Kayakers at dusk on Rye Pond in Stoddard. The pond is part of a protected supersanctuary. *Courtesy of Meade Cadot.*

Opposite, middle: Aerial shot of Spoonwood Pond and Nubanusit Lake on the border of Hancock and Nelson. *Courtesy of Eric Aldrich/TNC.*

Opposite, bottom: Altar of the Nations at Cathedral of the Pines features historic stones from all over the world. *Courtesy of Douglas Bryar.*

This page, top: Glacial boulders appear both above and below the surface at Willard Pond. *Courtesy of Lucie Bryar.*

This page, bottom: The Maple Guys in Lyndeborough, like most small maple producers, open their doors to visitors when the sap is running. *Courtesy of Douglas Bryar.*

Purgatory Brook Falls in Milford is not far from busy Route 101. *Courtesy of Douglas Bryar.*

Ducks sit on a dock at Lake Potanipo, at one time the site of the world's largest icehouse. *Courtesy of Lucie Bryar.*

Poet Robert Frost drew inspiration from this Derry farm during the ten years his family lived here. *Courtesy of Lucie Bryar.*

Stone walls line many back roads in southern New Hampshire, including this one in Walpole. *Courtesy of Jeffrey Newcomer, Partridgebrook Reflections.*

Opposite, top: Near St. Paul's School in Concord, Turkey Pond offers a quiet spot to canoe or kayak. *Courtesy of Lucie Bryar.*

Opposite, middle: You don't get this view driving by. Up close with lily pads and purple pickerel rush on Turkey Pond. *Courtesy of Lucie Bryar.*

Opposite, bottom: Deer are more common in the region since mountain lions and wolves have all but disappeared. *Courtesy of Denise Hurt.*

This page, top: Fringed polygala, also known as gaywings, is one of many wildflowers seen at Beaver Brook in Hollis. *Courtesy of Denise Hurt.*

This page, bottom: Following an extensive cleanup in the 1970s, the Nashua River today is home to abundant wildlife. *Courtesy of Lucie Bryar.*

Christmas tree farm on a Litchfield back road. *Courtesy of Douglas Bryar.*

Eastern painted turtles can be seen in the Nashua River and many other waterways in southern New Hampshire. *Courtesy of Denise Hurt.*

Look down on forest floors in New Hampshire to spot red efts, the terrestrial midlife stage of the red-spotted newt. *Courtesy of Denise Hurt.*

Adams Point, a peninsula between Little Bay and Great Bay, is a good spot to see bald eagles in winter. *Courtesy of Lucie Bryar.*

There's an easy boat launch for the Exeter River at Gilman Park. *Courtesy of Lucie Bryar.*

Portsmouth Harbor Lighthouse was the first lighthouse north of Boston when originally built in 1791. *Courtesy of Douglas Bryar.*

You can sail the Piscataqua River on a historic ship launched out of Portsmouth Harbor by the Gundalow Company. *Courtesy of Ralph Morang.*

Above: View of south Portsmouth from Peirce Island. The *Piscataqua*, a replica gundalow, was first launched from here in 2012. *Courtesy of Lucie Bryar.*

Left: Visitors to Star Island light candles each night in Gosport Chapel, keeping with a centuries-old tradition. *Author's collection, published by Hugh C. Leighton Co.*

Take this inviting walk across open fields and forests in any season. When you reach the end of the trail at Carter Hill Orchard, you will find a beautiful hilltop destination apple orchard, with views of seven New Hampshire mountains from its observation tower. In the fall, you can pick apples, of course, and you can also take part in an active raptor identification program offered by the New Hampshire Audubon Society. Experts are on site to help you decide if you're looking at a hawk or a vulture, and on announced days, they bring raptors for show and tell and occasionally release them into the wild.

With the absence of motorized vehicles, the West End Farm Trail is perfect for snowshoeing and cross-country skiing (ski rentals are available from the Capital Ski and Outing Club located in the barn). Snowshoers are asked to stay off the groomed trails and encouraged to blaze their own trails across the property.

In the Halls of St. Paul's

Are you a little curious about St. Paul's School, the major landowner in this corner of Concord? In fact, the campus of St. Paul's covers 2,000 acres, including almost all the land surrounding both Turkey Ponds and the upper third of the Turkey River. The Audubon Society of New Hampshire manages 680 acres of their property, making it accessible for walking and biking.

The private boarding school was founded in 1856 by Dr. George Cheyne Shattuck Jr., a Boston physician who donated his summer home. Since its founding, the school has changed in one important aspect—it began admitting girls in 1971—but it has held steadfast in another: St. Paul's remains today as one of only a handful of "all-boarding" schools in the country, meaning there are no day students here. Both students and faculty live nine months of the year at the school.

Some famous alumni have graduated from St. Paul's School. Among them are U.S. secretary of state John Kerry, film and television actor Efrem Zimbalist Jr., Pulitzer Prize–winning cartoonist Gary Trudeau, newspaper publisher and congressman William Randolph Hearst and co-founder of the Waldorf Astoria Hotel John Jacob Astor IV. While most of them were not contemporaries—from this list, only John Jacob Astor and William Randolph Hearst spent time here together—it's fun to imagine them all here at the same time. What stories the halls of St. Paul's could tell!

21

Nashua River Cleanup and the Power of One Woman

What I wanted to do was to make a difference in the world—which is what we all want to do—and can do.
—Marion Stoddart, national award-winning environmentalist and activist

In the 1950s, '60s and into the mid-'70s, the Nashua River was a polluted mess. Many longtime residents remember riding by the river with their car windows up, holding their noses from the stench—it smelled so strongly like rotten eggs that it began to affect property values and even drove away potential businesses.

The color of the water varied on any given day, from a dark rust to a bright yellow, depending on which dyes and inks had been dumped into the water by the paper industries that week. Many of us didn't know it at the time, but the Nashua River—named one of the top-ten dirtiest rivers in the country—was biologically dead.

It wasn't always that way. When Native Americans first came to the area about seven thousand years ago, the river—which flows thirty-seven miles north from Lancaster, Massachusetts, before emptying into the Merrimack River at Nashua—was clean and teeming with fish. They named it "Nash-a-way," meaning "river with the pebbled bottom," which leads us to believe they could actually see the bottom.

All that started to change with the Industrial Revolution beginning in the mid-1800s. That's when mills in both New Hampshire and Massachusetts started dumping industrial waste into the Nashua River, and many towns even discharged raw sewage into the water. Years of neglect only made the problem worse.

Today, the Nashua River is almost healthy again. It is a recreational asset to the area, and its waters and watershed are home to abundant wildlife. Plans are in the works for an expanded riverwalk in Nashua and a new boat launch will soon be added to the one that already exists. It's a remarkable turnaround story representing decades of hard work by many people, but most notably the work of one woman: Marion Stoddart.

In 1962, when Marion and her family moved to Groton, Massachusetts, the river was designated Class U, which is unsuitable for the transport of waste. Yet it didn't take long for this young housewife and mother to choose the river as her "project." Why would an ordinary citizen take on the monumental task of cleaning up a river that was so filled with solid sludge that it was said squirrels could walk across it?

"Wherever I lived, I always made it a point to assess the community's needs and decide what I could do to make a difference," says Marion, now eighty-five. "I purposefully chose the challenge of restoring the Nashua River because I felt it was accomplishable in my lifetime."

Growing up in the desert state of Nevada, Marion had learned to appreciate the "preciousness of water" from a young age. As an adult, she got involved with the League of Women Voters (LWV), which at the time was devoted to land and water issues. Through LWV, Marion honed her research, political and advocacy skills.

Her original goal was to address the river's watershed first. "It was my belief, then and now, that we could not maintain high water quality unless we protected its frontage from development," she says today.

To her credit, Marion was able to set her personal wishes aside when another group—the Conservation Commission in Hollis—got the attention of Governor Wesley Powell with a letter titled "Project Pure Water." In the letter, six hundred petitioners protested the condition of the river and asked the governor to join with the state of Massachusetts in a cleanup.

"Timing is everything, and I knew this was the moment in our country's history when we needed to get serious about our polluted rivers," Marion says. There were many challenges ahead. When Marion began her work, the Environmental Protection Agency had not yet been formed and the Clean Water Act had not yet been passed.

Undaunted, Marion got busy and formed the Nashua River Clean-Up Committee (now the Nashua River Watershed Association). She did hours of research, worked with people who shared similar goals and met with many state, regional and national leaders—sometimes privately and sometimes in well-publicized public forums. Occasionally, she would bring along a jar of dirty river water.

The turning point, says Marion, came at a public hearing held in 1967 by the Massachusetts Division of Water Pollution Control. Nashua River Clean-Up Committee members had decided that they would ask for the river to be restored to Class B—suitable for fishing, swimming, irrigation and boating. It was a bold move, considering the river was still considered "unsuitable for the transport of waste" at the time. They made the decision that "it was *our* river and we could have what we wanted if we asked for it," says Marion.

The group won a major victory when the state of Massachusetts agreed to improve the river to a B- in some sections and a C+ classification in others. "This meant that all treatment plants had to be redesigned or constructed in the next five years to meet those classifications," says Marion.

She recalls that very shortly after the new waste treatment plants began to operate, under the watchful eye of the newly formed Environmental Protection Agency, there was a dramatic improvement in the river. "[It seemed like] the river looked horrible one day and beautiful the next. Nature has a wonderful way of healing once we stop polluting."

At age "eighty-five, going on eighty-six," Marion is still hard at work on the Greenway Plan for the Nashua River, though she says, "I don't have a lot of time left and there's still much to be done."

She has won numerous awards for her work, including the prestigious United Nation's Environmental Programme's Global 500, which recognizes activists worldwide who have succeeded in the face of many obstacles. Three years ago, Marion was featured in *The Work of 1,000*, a documentary about her life and the river clean-up. "I've been appearing with the film and encouraging people to protect their rivers and to make a difference in the world," she says.

You can kayak or canoe the Nashua River in New Hampshire from a put-in near Stellos Stadium, off exit 5 from the Everett Turnpike. The river is home to a pair of territorial mute swans, Eastern Painted turtles, beavers, muskrats, osprey and lots of other wildlife. Be aware that mute swans guard a large territory of four to ten acres. While you might be tempted to get close, you really should give them plenty of space—especially when there are cygnets involved—since the adult swans here have been known to be aggressive.

Nashua River Rail Trail

Although more than 90 percent of the Nashua River Rail Trail is in Massachusetts, it's included in *Exploring Southern New Hampshire* because this outdoor treasure has its northernmost trailhead in Nashua, on Gilson Road just off Route 111. This well-used and well-loved trail is worth checking out for several reasons: the ten-foot-wide paved trail is relatively flat, making it an easy ride for those who enjoy this type of trail; it offers a variety of scenery and wildlife; and has well-marked road crossings and some nice off-trail stops. The trail from Nashua to Ayer, Massachusetts, is twelve and a half miles long.

The Nashua River Rail Trail roughly follows the Nashua River on what was once a Boston and Maine train route from Worcester to Nashua and then on to Portland, Maine. The first part of the rail line—from Worcester to Nashua—opened in 1848 and the second part, from Nashua to Portland, opened in 1874. Passenger service ended on the line in 1934, and the last freight train came through in 1982.

As you ride or walk the trail, you can still see some granite mile markers from the railroad era. A group called the Friends of the Nashua River Rail Trail renumbered the markers just as they would have appeared a century ago. Southbound, the markers have a "W" for Worcester, while northbound, they have a "P" for Portland. Before the days of radio communication, these mile markers let the train crews know exactly where they were on the line.

The Nashua River Rail Trail is used by walkers, bikers, inline skaters and, in winter, cross-country skiers. A section of the trail, from Pepperell to Groton, has a five-foot gravel shoulder for equestrians.

As you head out from the Nashua trail head, you'll soon come to a wetlands area that is a nice spot for bird and wildlife sightings. Look for beavers, herons and turtles. In Pepperell center, just off the trail, there's a Rail Trail ice cream shop that is a popular stop in summer. Continue on the trail toward Ayer, and you will come upon a variety of wetlands, marshes and woodlands.

Some rail trails are boring, but that's not the case with the Nashua River Rail Trail. There are several different natural features here, and you are guaranteed to see wildlife of some sort—even if it's only a snapping turtle lumbering across your path. Even those who are not up for a long bike ride will enjoy taking a short walk on this family-friendly trail.

PART III

The Seacoast

· ·

New Hampshire's Seacoast Region is small—it's about one-third the size of the Monadnock Region and half the size of the Merrimack Valley—but it's a region teeming with history, charm and a diverse landscape, including (at eighteen miles) the shortest coastline in the country. Here you'll find the cities of Dover and Portsmouth and twenty-seven small towns, many of them with a connection to the waters of the Atlantic or Great Bay Estuary.

On Route 1A, there's Hampton Beach, a resort area for more than one hundred years, marked by a crowded and noisy boardwalk with places to buy saltwater taffy and fried dough in the summer. But come here during the off-season, and it's a whole different story. As you gaze out into the foggy mist at the Isles of Shoals, located six miles out at sea, there's a sense of peace. You can drive the winding shore road north, or better yet, get out of your car and explore Little Boar's Head Walk on foot for stunning views of fishing shacks backed by sea spray on one side and sprawling historic mansions on the other.

The Great Bay Estuary, a mix of seawater from the Gulf of Maine and fresh water from seven rivers, offers a variety of diverse habitats not found anywhere else in the state. University scientists conduct research here while residents and visitors come to boat, fish and explore the deep channels, mudflats and salt marshes. With more than 7,300 acres of open water in the estuary alone, it's not surprising that the region has a long and varied maritime history. You can experience a small piece of it for yourself on a historic gundalow ride on the Piscataqua River.

Speaking of history, this region's position on the eastern seaboard made it a hotbed of activity during the Revolutionary War. Many townspeople in places like Dover, Exeter, Portsmouth and Hampton—all early settlements dating to the 1600s—played pivotal roles in the fight for independence. There's no quick and easy telling of colonial- and Revolutionary War–era history from a Granite State perspective. While you'll find tidbits here, there's a whole lot more to the story still waiting to be discovered or rediscovered.

In *On-the-Road Histories: New Hampshire*, historian Russell Lawson writes, "New Hampshire wears its heart on its sleeve." It's true. In the Seacoast Region, there are hundreds of homes, meetinghouses and churches that remain largely unchanged from when they were first built in the late 1600s to the early 1700s. As a visitor from outside the state remarked, "Everything is so *old* here." Well, yes, it is, and for many of us, that's a big part of the charm.

22

Applecrest Farm Orchards:
"History Never Tasted So Good"

*R*enee Addario Evelyn of Exeter remembers grilling hot dogs and working in the fields at Applecrest Farm as a teenager in the early 1990s. When the farm owners invited people to enter the "Your Farm Story" contest for their 100th anniversary in 2013, Renee's winning essay painted a vivid picture. She recalled "the wafting sound-waves of bluegrass music…the loud grumbling of tractors coming to a slow stop…the smell of everything cooking, roasting, baking, boiling…the colored blur of children running, racing, darting, jumping."

Through two years of high school and four years of college, Renee returned to work at the farm each year. "I carried and dug and weeded and landscaped and sorted and cut and baked," she recalls. Never mind that she endured sore feet, dirty clothes and strawberry juice–stained, callused hands, she did it all with a sense of pride and ownership: "Those were my hot dogs, my planted and weeded flower beds, my perfectly stacked bags of apples and my cut fruit for pies." Renee says the people she met here—particularly the stern but wise family matriarch, Imogen "Jeanie" Wagner—shaped and inspired her, instilling her with confidence in her own abilities and a strong work ethic.

Applecrest Farm is just that type of place—once you visit or work here, it seems to stay with you for a lifetime. People bring their children and then their grandchildren to the farm in Hampton Falls to create new memories year after year. The celebrated author John Irving, who worked here as a farmhand in the 1960s, even set some scenes in one of his novels at

Applecrest. Irving was just a typical teenager when he came to pick apples at the farm, yet this is the apple orchard that inspired some scenes in his bestselling book *Cider House Rules*, which later became a movie.

The Apple Train Stops Here

The story of Applecrest Farm is the story of the Wagner family, going back four generations. Todd Wagner is a third generation farmer who now operates the 220-acre farm with his father, Peter. Back in the 1980s, Peter had the vision to transform the farm into a fun-filled outdoor destination for families; the decision to diversify into "agritainment" made the farm less dependent on wholesale fruit prices and has turned out to be a big success.

Each weekend in the fall, there are harvest festivals with blue grass music, horse-drawn hayrides, pie-eating contests, face painting and, of course, the chance to pick your own apples, raspberries, peaches and pumpkins, eat homemade ice cream and indulge in old-fashioned apple cider donuts. Special events include an antique tractor pull in the fall. "We get our fields plowed and the East Coast Antique Tractor Club's aficionados get to drive their equipment," says Todd.

It's not all about entertainment, of course. Applecrest remains a true working farm, producing more than forty varieties of apples, tree-ripened peaches, nectarines, strawberries, blueberries, raspberries, sweet corn and many summer vegetables. It has a community-supported agriculture program and will soon open an on-site farm-to-table restaurant overlooking the orchards.

It all started when Peter's parents, Imogen "Jeanie" and William "Bill" Wagner, purchased the property from William Farmer in 1913. While Farmer waited seven years for his first apple trees to bear fruit, he ran a thriving chicken farm.

When the property turned over to the Wagner family in 1913, the full-fledged apple orchard was born, earning Applecrest Farm the distinction of being the oldest continuously operated apple orchard in the country today. The senior Wagners took advantage of the nearby Boston and Maine railroad station, both to bring their produce to market and to bring in "pick-your-own" enthusiasts. "My grandfather would drive to the rail station and pick up people from the Boston area who wanted to get out in the country," says Todd.

Both Todd and his father pursued other careers for a time—Todd in filmmaking and Peter in business—before being drawn back to the family farm. Peter says, "My wife and I decided it wasn't a bad way to raise a family…to live our lives…being outdoors and feeding the world with apples." Todd agrees. He now lives in the same house where his grandparents once lived and says, "I like the connection to history. It gives me a sense of place."

23

Great Bay:
New Hampshire's Hidden Coast

*A*t just 18 miles, New Hampshire has the smallest coastline in the country—of those states having a coastline, of course. But let's not forget that the Great Bay Tidal Estuary adds another 144 miles to our shoreline. It's easy to overlook the beauty and the recreational possibilities of the bay, in part because some of the shore is privately owned and off-limits. But there is still much to explore from many different vantage points in places like Dover, Durham, Greenland, Newmarket, Portsmouth and Stratham.

When we talk about the Great Bay coastline, we're not talking about soft-sand beaches and boardwalks lined with arcades. We are talking instead of an eleven-thousand-acre habitat made up of eelgrass beds, mudflats, tidal creeks, rocky shores, forests and meadows. Each one of these habitats is beautiful and inviting in its own way.

There are more than seven thousand acres of water in Great Bay—a mix of salt water from the Gulf of Maine and fresh water from seven rivers: the Lamprey, Squamscott, Winnicut, Cocheco, Salmon Falls, Bellamy and Oyster Rivers. Like all estuaries, Great Bay is a mix of tidal and fresh water. Twice each day, the Atlantic Ocean carries salt water into the bay, which means at varying times the water is fresh, brackish or salty.

The bay was formed by melting glaciers nearly fourteen thousand years ago, when a mile-high glacier from the Arctic carved out a river valley here. When the glaciers melted, the Atlantic Ocean rose and flooded the valley, creating the estuary. Starting at the mouth of the Piscataqua River between

Kittery, Maine, and New Castle, New Hampshire, the tidal waters travel fifteen miles inland before emptying into Great Bay near Hilton Point in Dover. It's one of the most recessed estuaries in the country.

Site of Proposed Oil Refinery

Great Bay is beautiful and protected today, but it was almost lost forever in 1973 and 1974. That's when billionaire shipping magnate Aristotle Onassis first revealed plans to build the world's largest oil refinery here. If he had succeeded, 3,500 acres along the shore of Great Bay would have been torn up to build a $600 million refinery. Tankers would have offloaded 400,000 barrels of crude oil each day into a giant pipeline at the Isles of Shoals.

In truth, Onassis and Olympic Oil didn't actually reveal their plans to townspeople near the seacoast. Instead, they hired outside realtors to approach people in Durham to sell off their land under a pretense. Some landowners were told it was for a nature preserve while others were told it was for a housing development. One thousand acres had already been sold off before Phyllis Bennett, the publisher of a small local newspaper, exposed Onassis' plan.

What followed was an epic "David and Goliath" battle. On one side was Onassis with "wads of money." He was backed by then New Hampshire governor Meldrim Thomson Jr. and William Loeb, the state's most conservative and powerful newspaper publisher. On the other side were three women with not much power or money, but with the strong belief that Great Bay should be protected as a regional treasure.

Phyllis Bennett was joined in her fight to stop Olympic Oil by two other women: Nancy Sandberg, then a twenty-seven-year-old Durham housewife, and Dudley Dudley, a state representative from Durham. Together they started a grass-roots "Save Our Shores" campaign.

The fierce battle that ensued was not so much about environmental issues as it was about who had the right to decide what would become of Great Bay. While one thousand people in Durham rallied to vote against the refinery, their vote was nonbinding. Nearby, voters in Rye had also turned down a proposal for a refinery.

Following those votes, Dudley Dudley acted quickly to introduce a Home Rule Bill (HB18) at a special session of the state legislature that would give Durham and other towns the right to decide what would happen in their own backyards. When Dudley's fellow New Hampshire legislators embraced Home Rule, the town of Durham told Onassis and Olympic Oil to go away.

It's easy for each succeeding generation to forget stories of political will and commitment like this that shaped our landscape. We can't really blame younger generations if they ask, "Aristotle who?" And Phyllis, Nancy and Dudley will probably never make it into the history books.

A small group of people, however, are trying to keep the "Onassis versus Durham" story alive. In 2011, they placed a large granite bench at Wagon Hill Farm in Durham by the waters of Little Bay. Carved from rock quarried in Milford by master stonecutter Steve Green, the bench is inscribed simply with the words, "Durham Says No to Olympic Oil Refinery."

Ed Valena, a driving force behind the massive granite bench, is trying to prevent the story from becoming a fading memory. He hopes when future visitors to Wagon Hill discover the curious inscription in the rock, they will use their mobile devices to get more information online.

Exploring the Bay by Boat

There are at least twenty-four boating access sites to the bay, each offering a different experience. According to the Great Bay National Estuarine Research Reserve, "The large waters that move in and out of the estuary create some of the strongest tidal currents in America." But don't fear. You can still enjoy quiet water canoeing or kayaking in Great Bay if you do some research first.

First, you need to find out the timing of high and low tides for the exact location where you plan to launch; just checking the posted tides in the local newspaper won't do. Tides can vary up to one and a half hours from one end of the bay to the other.

Great Bay offers another unique challenge for boaters. At low tide, more than half of the estuary drains completely and becomes one big mud flat. It's great if you are into soft-shelled clams, horseshoe crabs and wading birds. But it's not so great if you end up dragging your boat across the mud flats, sinking as you go.

This phenomenon—when about half of the bay drains like a bathtub twice a day—creates a dynamic natural show that is not seen anywhere else in the state. In a short span of just thirty to forty minutes, some sections of the bay transform from calm, shallow waters to thick mud.

The author kayaking Great Bay. You need to time your launch carefully since many sections turn to mud during low tide. *Courtesy of Douglas Bryar.*

It's a reminder that Mother Nature is in charge and if we want to play here, we should pay attention.

If you are not experienced in tidal waters, you can take a guided paddle with trained naturalists at the Great Bay Discovery Center in Greenland. Even if you choose to go it alone, the experts at the Discovery Center can advise you about the best time to launch from here. This site only accommodates car-top boats and is only accessible at high tide. Other popular launch sites are at Adams Point in Durham (mid- to high tide only) and Chapman's Landing (all tides), located on Route 108 on the Stratham/Newfields border.

With wide expanses of open water, small marshy creeks and mostly undeveloped shores, Great Bay offers a wonderful opportunity to see wildlife. You might spot muskrats, white-tailed deer, cottontail rabbits, otters and red foxes, to name a few. Birders will love it here, too, since the bay's position on the Atlantic Flyway makes it a stopping point for more than sixty different species of waterfowl, shorebirds and wading birds.

At the Discovery Center

You don't need a boat to enjoy the beauty of Great Bay. There are several walking trails, research sites and an education center. The Discovery Center's "Passport to Great Bay"(greatbay.org) is an excellent online guide for all ages, but a "must-have" if you want to get the most out of exploring Great Bay with children or grandchildren.

With its natural history displays and touch tank, the Discovery Center itself is a great starting point to learn about the bay. The center has a short 1,700-foot accessible boardwalk through a mixed habitat that opens up to wide open views of the bay. This area is known for its neotropical migrant birds—those that breed and raise their young in the north in the summer and then head south to tropical climates in the winter. They include warblers, tanagers, thrushes, sandpipers, plovers, teals and many more.

No other bird in North America has the rich blood-red body and jet-black wings and tail of the breeding male tanager. Be on the lookout for this colorful bird high in the treetops lining the boardwalk. Once the male tanager breeds and then molts, its plumage becomes a mix of green, yellow and red patches. By the time it begins its journey back to South America in the fall, the male is a dull green and yellow similar to the female.

Researchers Dive the Bay

Adams Point in Durham, a peninsula separating Little Bay and Great Bay, is considered one of the best spots to view bald eagles in winter; as many as a dozen eagles have been tracked here in recent years. This eighty-acre site has a one-and-a-half-mile walking and snowshoeing trail through oak-pine forests and along rocky shores and bluffs. It's also home to the University of New Hampshire's Jackson Estuarine Research Laboratory.

Helen Cheng, a graduate student in zoology, is part of a small group of researchers studying the American horseshoe crab from this lab. She explains that this is the northernmost range for this species—those born here stay in the estuary their entire lives, possibly because it's too far for them to crawl fifteen miles to the ocean. While adult crabs are easily spotted in summer, juvenile American horseshoe crabs are more difficult to find.

Helen Cheng conducts research on the American horseshoe crab in Great Bay. *Courtesy of Julian Russell, University of New Hampshire.*

"They are small and mobile and [we believe] they are around in the shallow mudflats which are difficult to access on foot without being waist-deep in mud," says Helen.

Intent on studying the juveniles, Helen and her colleagues scuba dive the estuary in the summer and early fall in search of the elusive baby crabs. Diving here can be scary and disorienting. "Because of its extensive and shallow mudflats and extreme currents, it is hard to gain a sense of direction, and you feel like you are swimming through chocolate milk," she says.

The young scientists' efforts are beginning to pay off, however. In 2012 and 2013, 110 juvenile horseshoe crabs were found, helping researchers to understand more about the critical habitats necessary for them to become adults.

Aside from studying horseshoe crabs, scientists at Adams Point delve into other organisms such as algae, seagrass and oysters. If you are interested in learning more about the work going on here, plan to attend the University's Ocean Discovery Day in the fall. Other UNH research sites open to the public, some of them year round, include one in New Castle that offers a tour of commercial fishing and research vessels and one in Durham that has a 120-foot-long wave tank.

Take a Hike in Great Bay Watershed

Another option to explore the bay's watershed on foot can be found on the Cy and Bobbie Sweet Trail, named for a husband and wife who have long been dedicated to protecting Great Bay. The four-mile-long trail begins on Longmarsh Road in Durham and continues through forests, freshwater wetlands and salt marshes before reaching Great Bay Estuary in Newmarket.

One of the highlights along the Sweet Trail is a giant beaver lodge on Crommet Creek. Be on the lookout, too, for nesting great blue herons, and watch in vernal pools for frogs and turtles. Some, like the Blanding turtle— identified by its helmet-shaped shell and bright yellow throat—are an endangered species in the state. Others, including the spotted turtle, are considered rare.

There's a bridge crossing Lubberland Creek from which you can see an active beaver slide. Apparently, the beavers use it to travel quickly between two ponds. At the end of the Sweet Trail, take a short walk to the Nature Conservancy's Great Bay office. The overlook here has a high-powered spotting scope that offers excellent views of a forty-acre grassland, thirty-acre salt marsh and the open waters of Great Bay.

The Great Bay National Wildlife Refuge, accessed from Pease Tradeport in Portsmouth, is yet another spot to get outdoors and see what you can see. You can explore two trails on foot or on snowshoes in winter, possibly spotting bald eagles or even snowy owls, which have appeared in larger than expected numbers on New Hampshire's seacoast recently.

Salt Marshes: Delicate Ecosystems in Need of Protection

Salt marshes are a beautiful but fragile part of our coastal landscape. Most of us love their swaying grasses, briny smell, flat meadows and meandering waters. A healthy salt marsh is one of the most productive ecosystems on the planet—it is very efficient at turning the sun's energy into plant life—but it takes a lot for a marsh to maintain its delicate balance.

Of the estimated 10,000 acres of salt marshes that existed in New Hampshire in colonial times, only about 6,200 acres survive today. Some of those remaining marshes have been "brought back to life" by conservationists working hard to restore them, particularly since the late 1990s. What happened to our salt marshes and what motivates people to save the salt marshes we have left?

First, a little history. When white settlers came to the New Hampshire seacoast from Massachusetts in the seventeenth and eighteenth centuries, they immediately saw the potential of the nutrition-rich grass produced by the marshes. Early farmers used the grass to feed their livestock and mulch their fields. They would begin harvesting the grass during low tides in August, at first hand-cutting it with scythes and, later, using horse-drawn cutting machines and eventually tractors.

Some salt marshes that were lost to development are being restored today. *Courtesy of Lucie Bryar.*

Unfortunately, the harvesting of marsh grass disturbed the delicate habitat in the marshes. If crustaceans, mollusks and birds depended on those grasses, where did they go when the grasses were cut down?

Fast-forward nearly three hundred years. With development going on in the seacoast, towns like Hampton, Rye, North Hampton and Greenland built coastal roads and culverts and dug ditches to drain the marshes. All of these things interrupted the tidal flow that is essential to a healthy marsh. The prevailing belief at one time was that marshes were simply breeding grounds for mosquitoes. We now know that draining marshes actually increases the mosquito population, because it depletes the fish that feed on mosquito larvae.

In the last two decades, many local, state and federal agencies have come together to actively restore and enhance New Hampshire's salt marshes. People now understand that healthy marshes play a role in the commercial fishing industry—they sustain small fish that serve as food for larger fish—and they also help to control storm surges from reaching populated areas. As you travel throughout the region, be on the lookout for healthy marshes, as well as those still overgrown with invasive species like purple loosestrife or narrow leaf cattails. Educate yourself about this important habitat, or better yet, get involved in a salt marsh restoration project. There is still work to be done!

24

In Lincoln's Footsteps:
Retrace His 1860 Visit to Exeter

*T*he town of Exeter is probably best known as the home of Phillips Exeter Academy, a prestigious prep school that was founded in 1781 by Dr. John Phillips. John's nephew, Samuel, had successfully founded Phillips Academy in Andover, Massachusetts, just three years before with the backing of his father and his uncles. John was apparently a bright man; he entered Harvard University at age eleven and was class salutatorian when he graduated at age fourteen in 1735.

As you might imagine for an institution with a history spanning more than 230 years, Phillips Exeter has a long list of notable alumni. New Hampshire's only president, Franklin Pierce, graduated from here, as did statesman and orator Daniel Webster. Many other alums went on to become governors, congressmen, authors and historians. In more contemporary times, accomplished graduates have included Greg Daniels, producer of the TV show *The Simpsons*, and Mark Zuckerberg, the founder of Facebook.

One person arguably with the highest name recognition among the long list of Phillips Exeter graduates is Robert Todd Lincoln, who enrolled in the academy after failing Harvard's entrance exam. His father came to visit him while he was a student here in 1860.

It's interesting to note that when Abraham Lincoln stepped off the train in Exeter in late February of that year, he had not yet received the Republican Party's nomination for president. In fact, historians disagree about his political aspirations at that time. If we back up just two weeks, we learn that Lincoln—an attorney and one-term congressman from Illinois

Robert Todd Lincoln in 1860, when he was a student at Phillips Exeter Academy. *Courtesy of Library of Congress.*

who had also lost a senate bid—originally planned to come to Exeter simply to spend time with his son.

But history had other ideas. Just three days before arriving in New Hampshire, Lincoln had given a triumphant speech in New York about limiting the expansion of slavery. News about his talk spread quickly and the reluctant "candidate" was bombarded with speaking requests from the moment he set foot in the Granite State. He wrote to his wife, Mary Todd Lincoln, that, "If I had foreseen it, I think I would not have come East at all."

During his two-week visit to New England, the future president spoke to standing-room-only crowds in Concord, Dover, Exeter, Manchester and other cities in the region. Some historians believe the momentum Lincoln gained in New Hampshire helped him to win the Republican nomination just three months later. Lincoln didn't rise from obscurity to national prominence based on that one speech in New York and a string of speeches in New England, however. He had gained national attention two years earlier during the infamous Lincoln-Douglas debates held during his senate run.

On the 150th anniversary of his visit to Exeter, the Exeter Historical Society released the Abraham Lincoln Walking Tour. Following this route is a great way to get outside in this small, history-filled town, where it's not so hard to imagine what it must have been like when Lincoln walked these same streets.

The first stop on the walking tour is the railroad station on Arbor Street where Lincoln disembarked from New York. A section of the original building still stands. At the time of Lincoln's visit, the train tracks passed right through the building. To get to his speaking engagement in Concord from here, Lincoln had to travel by way of Lawrence, Massachusetts, and then Manchester, New Hampshire. The forty-four-mile trip from Exeter to Concord that takes less than forty-five minutes today took three to four hours by train in Lincoln's day.

Next on the tour is the Amos Tuck House at 89 Front Street. This elegant Italianate-style house, still a private residence today, was home to U.S. congressman Amos Tuck. Tuck and Lincoln had become close friends during their freshman terms in Congress, and it was Tuck who convinced Lincoln to send his son to Phillips Exeter Academy.

For many years, it was believed that Lincoln slept at the Tuck House during his Exeter visit—there was even a historical marker saying so. But we now know this isn't true. A letter found in recent years revealed that Tuck was out of town during Lincoln's visit, and what's more, he was upset with Abe for not stopping in to visit his wife and daughter. No one knows for sure where Lincoln stayed during his visit to Exeter, though it was probably at a local inn.

We do know that Lincoln and Robert attended church services at the Second Parish Church that stood adjacent to Phillips Exeter Academy at that time. When the Second Parish Church merged with the First Parish Church in 1920 (now Exeter Congregational Church), the pew used by the Lincolns was moved to this building. You can sit in the pew today if you visit the church vestry during coffee hour following Sunday services.

When you are in downtown Exeter, it's hard to miss the small pavilion or bandstand in the center of town, another stop on the Historical Society's tour. This structure was designed by architect Henry Bacon, who also designed the Lincoln Memorial in Washington, D.C. Bacon often worked with renowned sculptor and Exeter native Daniel Chester French, though the two didn't collaborate on the bandstand.

French, who is perhaps best known for the Minuteman statue in Concord, Massachusetts, also sculpted the seated Lincoln statue in the Lincoln Memorial. You can see a local example of French's work in the elegant World War I Memorial that stands in Gale Park on Front Street. The sculptor's

The Swasey Bandstand in downtown Exeter was designed by architect Henry Bacon, who also designed the Lincoln Memorial. *Courtesy of Douglas Bryar.*

The Exeter Congregational Church now has the pew occupied by Abraham Lincoln and his son in 1860. *Courtesy of Douglas Bryar.*

A statue sculpted by Daniel Chester French stands in Exeter's Gale Park. French's most widely known statue is the Lincoln Memorial. *Courtesy of Douglas Bryar.*

birthplace on 24 Court Street is also part of the Exeter Historical Society's walking tour. To obtain the full walking tour, which includes eleven sites, visit exeternh.gov or contact the Historical Society.

Moving on from the Lincoln walking tour, head to Exeter's Great Falls and the Great Dam, accessed from String Bridge Street not far from the bandstand. This is the spot where the Exeter River and the Squamscott River meet. It should come as no surprise that this site played an important role in the establishment and growth of the town.

In 1638, Reverend John Wheelwright purchased land from the Algonquin Indians in order to establish a village here. Soon, the water was harnessed for gristmills, sawmills, carding mills, iron mills and paper mills. For the next two hundred years, Exeter was a thriving industrial community, with raw materials and finished products often transported back and forth by flat-bottomed boats called gundalows to large ocean-going vessels.

George Washington Was First President to Walk These Streets

History lovers could spend many hours, perhaps even days, in Exeter. We already know that Abe Lincoln came to this seaport town in 1860. But if we back up seventy-one years, we learn that George Washington rode his horse from Portsmouth to Exeter in the fall of 1789 as our country's newly inaugurated president.

Apparently Washington chose to ride alone instead of taking a carriage. While citizens in Stratham got word of his trip and lined the roadways to greet him, it was a different story in Exeter. According to an account by the Exeter Historical Society, "a planned calvacade of dignitaries failed to collect on time and it was left to Captain Simon Wiggin and his artillery company to greet the president with a 13-gun salute."

We don't know if Washington was relieved or disappointed that there were no dignitaries on hand to give speeches; no mention was made of it in his diary or his letters. But we're told that he promptly dismounted his horse and went to breakfast at Folsom's Tavern, located at that time on the corner of Front and Water Streets. The tavern has been moved three times and has served many purposes since it was first constructed around 1775. Today, you can find the historic building, which is now owned by the American Independence Museum, at 164 Water Street.

American History Treasures in Independence Museum

This museum possesses some true American treasures, including a rare Dunlap broadside of the Declaration of Independence as well as early drafts of the Constitution. If you want to see the originals, you'll have to time your visit precisely, however, since they are currently only on display one day a year during the museum's Independence Day Festival in mid-July.

When the members of the Continental Congress first adopted the Declaration of Independence on July 4, 1776, someone from the group took the handwritten document to John Dunlap's Philadelphia print shop. We don't know how many copies of the historic document Dunlap was asked to print, but only twenty-six of them are known to exist today. The one in Exeter was found as part of a collection—which included those early drafts of the Constitution—in the attic of the Ladd-Gilman House during renovations in 1985.

For protection, the original documents are stored off site in a secure and climate-controlled location. The museum hopes to "bring these items home," however, once they add climate control to the Ladd-Gilman House, according to Executive Director Julie Williams. Until then, you can view copies of the documents, along with many other historic artifacts, including an original Purple Heart awarded to a soldier by General George Washington. The museum, which includes the main building plus the Gilman-Ladd House and Folsom's Tavern, is open seasonally from May to November.

Exploring Exeter's Walking Trails and Rivers

Phillips Exeter Academy owns and maintains a network of walking trails open to the public. You can access one trailhead by turning right onto Water Street from the bandstand in downtown. Stay straight through the traffic light and follow High Street to Drinkwater Road on the right. The access gate is off Drinkwater Road on your right. You can also access some academy trails from Gilman Park on Bell Avenue.

It seems you can't escape history while you're in Exeter. If you take the Jude Pond loop from the academy's blue trail, you will come to a small pond that isn't all that impressive to look at, though you might see some Mallard ducks. Still, there's history here.

The pond and the loop trail are named for Jude Hall, a runaway slave who had a small homestead at this site. Hall, who enlisted in the Revolutionary War on the colonial side, fought in the Battle of Bunker Hill and is believed to have fought with distinction at Ticonderoga, in Trenton, at Saratoga and at Valley Forge. "Though he fought to free a nation," writes Barbara Kimkunas, "[Hall] was unable to see his own children become free." Hall spent many years trying to find and free three of his sons who were captured and enslaved. Jude Hall is buried in the town's Winter Street Burial Ground.

If you are interested in paddling the Exeter River, head to Gilman Park for an easy put-in. From this launch site, you can meander several miles on the narrow winding waterway. The tea-colored water has overhanging tree limbs, lending a somber feel to some parts. Other sections have shoreline development and road noise. Depending on where you launch and where you paddle, you can have a very different experience.

For another type of outing, you can canoe or kayak the tidal Squamscott River from Stratham to Swasey Park in Exeter. Start from the boat launch at Chapman's Landing on Route 108 near the town border between Stratham and Newfields. From the launch, head south for the Squamscott River; if you head north, you'll be paddling straight into Great Bay. To make the trip to Exeter, you'll need to time your launch with the tide coming in, about two hours before high tide, and time your return trip during the receding tide.

25

Fort Constitution and the First Midnight Ride of Paul Revere

By Douglas Bryar

*A*nyone who has studied American history is familiar with Longfellow's poem "Paul Revere's Ride," chronicling the patriot's journey from Boston to Lexington, Massachusetts, to warn the colonists that the British were headed their way in what was to be known as the first battle of the Revolutionary War. But fewer people know this was not Revere's first "midnight ride." The first ride actually took place four months earlier in December 1774—in frigid temperatures over icy roads—when Paul Revere rode to Portsmouth to sound the alarm that the British were coming to secure and reinforce the fort known as William and Mary.

Fort William and Mary had been built by the British in 1639 and was known at that time simply as "the castle." The fort was built to protect the Crown's interests in the colonies from other powers, most notably France. Many improvements were made to the fort over the years, and in the late 1600s, the fort was renamed William and Mary after the reigning monarchs of the time. Located at the mouth of the Piscataqua River on New Castle Island, the fort was of crucial importance to the early colonists since it was one of the main munitions depots for the colony.

In October 1774, after hearing of unrest in the colonies, King George III issued a confidential order forbidding the export of gunpowder or arms to America. Also fearing that the stockpiles that existed in the colonies might fall into colonists' hands, the king made plans to send troops to America to secure the depots. Somehow word of the plan reached the patriots in Boston, and as a result, Paul Revere made his midnight ride to Portsmouth on December 13, 1774. Once there, he met with Samuel Cutts of the local assembly at his Market Street home, where plans were quickly made to raid the fort and remove the munitions.

At around noon on December 14, Captain John Langdon, along with a drummer and fife, marched through the streets of Portsmouth sounding a call to arms. By the time they reached the fort by gundalow, their numbers had grown to about four hundred, including citizens from the neighboring towns of Rye and New Castle. (Imagine assembling a group this large so quickly in the days long before the invention of the telegraph or the telephone and centuries before social media.)

The fort at that time was manned by Loyalist captain John Cochran and five soldiers. At some point in the early afternoon, Cochran's group fired on the colonists with cannons and rifles, and fire was returned. Fortunately, no one was injured, and before a second volley could be fired, the fort was overtaken by the colonists and the king's colors were lowered.

The raid on Fort William and Mary netted the colonists about one hundred barrels of gunpowder that were quickly loaded onto gundalows and sent up the Piscataqua River, where they were dispersed to various towns.

Historic photo of Fort Constitution (originally named Fort William and Mary), one of seven forts built to protect Portsmouth Harbor. *Author's collection.*

Fort Constitution, in New Castle, seen today, has a long history dating back to pre–Revolutionary War days. *Courtesy of Douglas Bryar.*

The sitting royal governor at the time, Sir John Wentworth, was caught up in the tensions between the colonists and the Crown. Wentworth hastily requested British support in the form of troops and ships from Boston. On December 17, 1774, the English sloop *Canceaux* arrived, followed a couple days later by the English frigate *Scarborough*, which carried forty cannons and one hundred English marines, who reclaimed the fort.

Governor Wentworth remained in Portsmouth for several months while tensions continued to worsen. According to one account, in the spring of 1775, an unruly mob surrounded the governor's home in Portsmouth, pointing a cannon at his front door. The governor and his family made a hasty retreat out the back door, making their way to Fort William and Mary, which was still under British protection. The Wentworth family eventually resettled in Halifax, Nova Scotia.

If you would like to see the mansion where Sir John and his family were living when they were forced out by angry colonists, you can drive by the Mark Wentworth Home, today an assisted living facility, at 346 Pleasant Street in Portsmouth. The building is listed on the National Register of Historic Places and was established as a facility for invalids as early as 1900 by sixteenth-generation members of the Wentworth family.

Since so many generations of the Wentworth family played a pivotal role in New Hampshire's history, there are still several Wentworth mansions in the Portsmouth area. Best known among them is the Wentworth-Coolidge Mansion on Little Harbor Road, now a state park open to the public in the summer. The Wentworth who lived here was not Sir John, but rather his uncle Benning Wentworth, who was the state's first royal governor, from 1741 to 1766.

Visiting Fort Constitution and Portsmouth Harbor Lighthouse

Fort William and Mary was renamed Fort Constitution in 1791, after the State of New Hampshire turned it over to the United States government. One of seven forts built to protect Portsmouth Harbor, Fort Constitution has undergone renovations and repairs through the years, most recently in 2013.

The fortification wall you see today is twice as high as it was during colonial times, and the ruins you see here are remnants of a fort reconstruction in 1808. Beyond its role in the Revolutionary War, Fort Constitution was used during the War of 1812 and for training exercises during the Civil War. It also served limited roles in the Spanish-American War, World Wars I and II and, at one time, served to protect Portsmouth Naval Shipyard. The fort was given back to the state in 1961.

A historic marker at the site, placed here in 1802 by the Society of Colonial Wars–New Hampshire, heralds the efforts of Captain John Langdon, Major John Sullivan and their fellow colonists in what is termed "the first victory of the American Revolution." Some historians believe the fort deserves to be recognized as the spot where it all began, rather than Lexington and Concord, where the first casualty occurred.

Whichever viewpoint you adopt, you can sit outside in Portsmouth's Market Square today and look across the street to the towering spire of the North Church. Imagine Paul Revere charging through here on his horse late one night. If the clocks were turned back to 1774, would you join the ranks of colonists who followed the call of the drummer and fife on a cold December day to sail out to New Castle Island to overtake a fort? This one act alone is a subtle reminder that our nation was founded by ordinary citizens willing to commit extraordinary acts in the name of independence.

Adjacent to Fort Constitution is the historic Portsmouth Harbor Lighthouse overlooking the Atlantic Ocean. The lighthouse was built in 1771, making it

The North Church of Portsmouth was built in 1855. *Courtesy of Douglas Bryar.*

the first lighthouse in the American colonies north of Boston. It was rebuilt one hundred yards east in 1804 and rebuilt yet again in 1878, at that time in cast iron instead of wood. There are some fascinating stories surrounding the many lighthouse keepers who called Portsmouth Harbor Lighthouse home through the years. To learn more, you can visit the lighthouse when it's open on Sunday afternoons during the summer.

26

Downtown Dover:
Where Three Rivers Flow

*E*nglish explorers and Native Americans thousands of years before them were first attracted to Dover for its three rivers: the Piscataqua to the east (joining the area to the Atlantic Ocean) and the Bellamy and Cochecho Rivers flowing through what is now the center of town. The powerful Cochecho Falls, still a prominent feature in downtown, helped to bring the Industrial Revolution here in a big way.

While Dover has a lively, family-friendly feel today, the seacoast's largest city (population 30,220) hasn't strayed very far from its gritty working-class roots. You can still see the brick mill buildings lining Central Avenue, Main Street and Washington Street. They have all been repurposed now, but in the nineteenth century, the buildings were home to a number of large textile mills.

The Cocheco Mills of Dover, known at the time for their production of printed calico cloth, came into the national limelight in December 1828 as the site of the first women's strike in the country. According to a Dover Chamber of Commerce brochure, "[That year], new rules were enforced at the mills which forbade talking between employees during work hours, prohibited unions, imposed fines for being late and reduced wages from 58 cents to 53 cents a day." In protest, half of the women's eight hundred "mill girls" took to the streets, parading with banners and fireworks.

The local press was unsympathetic to the women. It even went so far as to describe the march as a "disgusting scene," according to the December 30, 1828 issue of the *Dover Enquirer*. When the mill owners advertised for four hundred replacement workers, the women returned to their jobs, but not before they had inspired other mill workers in the region to fight for change.

The following year, there were strikes in Taunton and Lowell, Massachusetts. But it would take nearly one hundred more years before striking mill workers would contribute to the demise of giants like the Amoskeag Manufacturing Company in Manchester. You can see a commemorative plaque about the Dover women's strike near the Cochecho Falls courtyard on Central Avenue.

Intrigue in the Cemetery

The chamber of commerce offers three self-guided Heritage Walking Tours developed by the Dover Historical Society. The tours focus on historic houses, the mills and the Pine Hill Cemetery. They are a good starting point, but any history lover looking for tales of betrayal and violent revenge—all prevalent in the early history of Dover—will need to do a little digging on his or her own.

When white settlers first came here in 1623, they peacefully coexisted with the Abenaki Indians for nearly half a century before tensions flared. Dover was the site of the bloody Cochecho Massacre in 1689 as well as a conflict called Father Rale's War in 1723. The following year, Dover resident Elizabeth Hanson was kidnapped by Native Americans and held for twenty-two months with some of her children in Canada before being rescued by her husband. You can read her intriguing firsthand narrative online in *An Account of the Captivity of Elizabeth Hanson*.

If you follow the Dover Historical Society's tour of Pine Hill Cemetery, located on East Watson Street off Central Avenue, you'll be directed to fourteen gravestones of interest. Some of them belong to sea captains, Revolutionary War veterans and villains, and there is one "weeping bride," which is hard to miss. As the story goes, Cordelia Teatherly was engaged to businessman Henry Law when he called off the wedding plans because she refused to get rid of her dog. Upon her death, Cordelia arranged to have a large stone monument erected with a crying woman sitting atop it. She left specific instructions to situate the statue with her back facing Henry Law's plot.

One person buried here but not mentioned in the chamber's brochure is Lucy Hale Chandler. Hers is a story filled with romance, national intrigue and possibly betrayal. The daughter of U.S. congressman John P. Hale of

Dover, Lucy was considered one of the belles of Washington, D.C. She had dated Robert Todd Lincoln briefly and remained longtime friends with him.

But it's her engagement to Lincoln assassin John Wilkes Booth that has raised much speculation from historians. There seems to be little doubt that Lucy was drawn to the handsome and well-known stage actor, but it's not clear if Booth's feelings for her were true. There is some evidence that he pursued her for her connections to Washington insiders so that he could attempt to carry out his plot to kidnap Lincoln.

Lucy had secured a ticket for Booth to Lincoln's second inauguration, and we also know she spent time with her beloved and with Robert Todd Lincoln on the day of the president's assassination. Did she inadvertently tip off Booth about the Lincolns' plans to attend a play at Ford Theater that night?

Lucy's father strongly opposed the romance between his daughter and Booth, who was an anti-abolitionist and a renowned lady's man. On the morning of the assassination, Senator Hale met with President Lincoln and asked to be appointed ambassador to Spain. Historians believe his motive was to take his daughter out of the country, away from her fiancé.

When Booth was finally captured in a barn in Virginia twelve days after the assassination, he had a photo of Lucy in his pocket, along with the photos of three other women. The story of John Wilkes Booth and Lucy Hale Chandler was dramatized in a 1998 made-for-TV movie *The Day Lincoln Was Shot*. Their relationship is also mentioned in the National Geographic documentary *Killing Lincoln*, released in 2013.

Dover's Wildlife Management Area

Leaving downtown Dover and the cemetery, you can find an outdoor spot with a more remote feel to it at the Bellamy River Wildlife Management Area, a 440-acre natural site managed by the New Hampshire Fish and Game Department. The nearby 26-acre Bellamy River Sanctuary is operated by New Hampshire Audubon.

Located on the western shore of the Bellamy River between Dover and Portsmouth, the wildlife management area offers trails through river shoreline, tidal creeks, forested areas and fields. Activities allowed here are hiking, cross-country skiing, snowshoeing, wildlife watching and hunting—with one exception.

It is illegal to hunt New England cottontail rabbits here since they are an endangered species in New Hampshire. In fact, this site is home to the largest New England cottontail habitat project in the state. Beginning in 2011, loggers clear-cut thirty acres of trees to allow young seedlings and saplings to spring up in their place. This "jungle of regrowing trees and shrubs" is an ideal habitat for rabbits to rest, as well as feed and raise their young, according to Fish and Game Department officials.

If you take time to walk the Clements Point Trail at the Audubon's wildlife sanctuary, you may see grassland birds (in season) in open fields before entering a shady forest. From the Cove Trail, you will enjoy views of intertidal habitat, Royalls Cove and the Bellamy River.

You can kayak or canoe the Bellamy River, heading upriver from the Scammell Bridge on Route 4 in Dover. Since this is a tidal river, it's best to paddle during high tide so that you'll have full access to all the tidal creeks. While there's occasional truck noise from the Spaulding Turnpike, one kayaker has called it "one of the best wilderness experiences in all of Great Bay." If you're a bird lover, you may want to time your trip in September, during the fall migration.

27

Little Boar's Head Walk
and History Along the Sea

Often, when the sunrise hits their windowpanes at the proper angle, the resulting rays sparkle and reflect back over the velvet lawns, formal gardens and old stone walls and continue to unlimited skies and wide vistas of the Atlantic Ocean. The more we see these mansions, the more they seem to improve with age.
—*North Hampton resident Ken Palm, writing for* Rye Reflections

For eighteen miles, the New Hampshire portion of Route 1A hugs the coastline, starting in Seabrook and heading north through parts of Hampton, Hampton Beach, North Hampton and Rye before coming to an end in downtown Portsmouth. For much of the route, the open waters of the Atlantic are in full view.

During the summer, beachgoers often find themselves caught in traffic on this busy road. Some choose instead to visit during the off-season or on a rainy day, when they can drive through at a more leisurely pace to gaze at the beautiful stately mansions facing the ocean.

Instead of driving by, consider getting out of your car and taking a stroll along Little Boar's Head Walk, a one-and-a-half-mile district in North Hampton that is on the National Register of Historic Places. When you walk, you can inhale the seaweed-scented air, feel the ocean breeze on your face and pause long enough to consider some of the history behind the mansions and the landscape.

To find Little Boar's Head Walk, make your way to North Hampton State Beach, across the road from the Beach Plum restaurant, which boasts it has

Little Boar's Head Walk begins near a row of fishing houses once used by commercial fishermen. *Courtesy of Dennis King.*

some of the best ice cream in the United States. You'll find the start of the walkway on the north end of the beach parking lot near a stretch of ten fishing houses. Built mostly in the 1800s, these small houses served at one time as working fish houses for residents of North Hampton before being turned into seaside retreats.

Continuing on, you'll pass a large rock engraved with a poem written in 1944 by a member of the Navy Patrol Bombing Squadron. You are now at a bluff called Little Boar's Head. On a clear day, look out to sea at the Isles of Shoals—nine rocky and barren islands that are divided between New Hampshire and Maine. It is said the fish were so plentiful here during the 1600s that you could "walk to the mainland on the backs of the cod."

It's a far different story today. The fish have greatly diminished from the days when the islands served as fishing camps for Native Americans and early settlers. Only some of the islands are accessible for day trips on a limited basis. You may be able to book passage on a University of New Hampshire research vessel that makes regular trips to Appledore Island (owned by Maine).

You can also take a day trip to Star Island, the largest of the New Hampshire–owned islands, on a cruise offered by the Isles of Shoals

Steamship Company in Portsmouth. The main features on Star Island are an overnight conference center operated by the Unitarian Universalist Church and Gosport Chapel, which sits on the highest point of land. The chapel you see here today was built in 1800, though it was preceded by a number of other buildings built as early as 1685.

Before a lighthouse came to this region (135 years after the first church), it was the daily custom of the people living in this thriving fishing village to go up to the little church at night. There, they would pray for the fishermen whose boats had not returned that day and they would hang lanterns from wooden crosses on the walls. They hoped their lights would guide the men at sea safely back to port. This touching and solemn tradition, dating back at least three centuries, still takes place on the island today.

Summer Home to the Wealthy

As you continue on Little Boar's Head Walk, you'll see several large historic "summer cottages" with deep lawns and lush landscaping. This area, originally a farming and fishing community, had become a summer colony by the mid-1800s. There was a large resort hotel, the Bachelder, along with several rental cottages and the magnificent private homes we see today. Most of the homes were designed by prominent architects of the day for wealthy politicians and businessmen.

A number of presidents, congressmen, cabinet members and governors summered at Little Boar's Head. Among them were Franklin Pierce—the state's only president—as well as Presidents James Garfield, Chester Arthur, William Taft and Franklin Delano Roosevelt. Robert Todd Lincoln summered here when he was secretary of state. Of these, only Pierce built a home in North Hampton.

You can still see the stately Studebaker mansion, built in 1874, at 40 Ocean Boulevard. In 1909, the home was purchased by Ada Studebaker of South Bend, Indiana. Her husband, George, was an executive with the Studebaker Corporation, founded by his father and his uncles. Starting out as a manufacturer of horse-drawn wagons, the company went on to become one of the most successful automotive companies in the country, from about 1912 until its closing in 1966.

Reportedly, George and Ada had a sixty-four-room mansion in South Bend and this 8,550-square foot summer home in North Hampton. George's

George Studebaker and his wife owned this summer "cottage" in North Hampton until they lost their fortune in the Great Depression. *Courtesy of Dennis King.*

brother Clement (some say the family member was a cousin) also built an eighteen-room home in nearby Rye—so occasionally there is confusion when people talk about the "Studebaker Home" on the seacoast.

George and Clement grew up in a well-to-do family, and as Studebaker executives, both became multimillionaires in their own right. But the two men lived out their final years very modestly, after both suffered financial ruin in the Great Depression. They lost their fortunes to a bad investment with the Samuel Insull utilities empire. Insull, a close associate of Thomas Edison, was the first to introduce metered electric service in the United States. Unfortunately, he sold a large number of cheap stocks and bonds that became worthless.

George Studebaker sold his home in North Hampton in 1936 and declared bankruptcy. He and his wife, Ada, were also forced to give up their mansion in South Bend along with their household servants. Years after the Studebaker's sold the Ocean Boulevard mansion, it was sold again to the Costello family, owners of the *Lowell Sun* newspaper.

Moving on, you'll come to Willow Avenue on the left, where you can visit Fuller Gardens, a turn-of-the-century botanical garden open to the public from May to October. The two-and-a-half-acre property has thousands of rose bushes, formal English perennial borders and a Japanese garden.

The garden was established in 1927 by Alvan T. Fuller, a self-made businessman, philanthropist and politician from the Boston area. He had the gardens built for his wife, Viola. It is said the two rarely stepped outside into the garden, though they enjoyed the view from their summer mansion (now demolished).

Fuller made his fortune in the car business, selling Packards and Cadillacs. He had his start in the business at age twenty-one, when he traveled to Europe and brought back the first two cars to enter the port of Boston: two French De Dion–Bouton Voiturettes.

In 1914, at the urging of Theodore Roosevelt, Fuller began his political career, serving two terms in the Massachusetts legislature and two terms in Congress before being elected governor of Massachusetts. He never cashed a paycheck as a public servant. It's interesting to note that while Fuller was governor of the Bay State, his summer home in North Hampton sat right next door to New Hampshire governor Huntley Spaulding's summer home. Today, the two states enjoy a healthy competition for businesses and retail shoppers; we have to wonder if the two governors at that time had backyard barbecues or possibly long talks over the garden fence.

28

Historic Gundalows:
Ride the Tide, Sail the Winds

*Y*ou can read about the gundalow—a unique boat that played a key role in this region from the 1600s to the 1800s—or you can set sail on one and feel history start to come alive. In 2012, after a decade of planning, designing and fundraising, a new gundalow named the *Piscataqua* was finally launched from Peirce Island in Portsmouth to the cheers of hundreds of supporters and onlookers.

The historic reproduction was built from a temporary shipyard at Strawbery Banke by a team of master boat builders from New Hampshire and Maine. Their challenge was to design a boat that would both pay tribute to the original gundalows and, at the same time, meet today's U.S. Coast Guard safety regulations for seaworthiness. And so they used big oak planks from Massachusetts, pine from fallen trees along the Cochecho River and metal parts hand-forged by a Portsmouth blacksmith; but for safety, they also added an engine, lifelines and watertight bulkheads.

What is a gundalow exactly, and why build a new one today? Gundalows were shallow-drafted, flat-bottomed cargo barges once common in the Gulf of Maine's rivers and estuaries. In the early days, the boats had no decks and were poled or rowed using long oars called sweeps. Over time, a lateen sail was added so that the wind could be used for navigation when the tides or currents weren't cooperating. The sails were designed to go up and down quickly so the barges could easily navigate under bridges.

There was nothing pretty about the early gundalows. They were simple workhorses, often built by farmers using timber from their own woodlots.

The boats were used to move farm produce, bricks, hay, firewood, granite, coal and iron, as well as raw materials for the mills up and down the hundreds of miles of interconnecting inland waterways on New Hampshire's seacoast.

Gundalows had to be able to carry heavy loads in the fast-running deep waters of the tidal Piscataqua River and in its much shallower, slower tributaries. And by all accounts, they did their job quite well for nearly three hundred years. Then the railroads came in and replaced them because, quite simply, trains could operate at faster speeds in all seasons, even when the rivers were iced over.

Ship with a Mission: Connecting People to Place

The new *Piscataqua* serves today as a sailing classroom for the nonprofit Gundalow Company, founded in 1999. Their mission is "to protect the Piscataqua region's maritime heritage and environment through education and action."

Since launching in 2012, the historic barge has offered educational programs for thousands of students, as well as many public sailing trips for adults during the summer months. In essence, the boat replaced the *Captain Adams*, a thirty-year-old reproduction gundalow that was often docked at the Great Bay Discovery Center. Because the *Adams* was never designed to be sailed, students had to be rowed out in a skiff to hop onboard for a lesson.

Molly Bolster, executive director of the Gundalow Company, had a different vision for the historic boats since she came on board in 2002. As she watched kids and adults being taught dockside about the Piscataqua's maritime history, she says, "I knew from the beginning that we had to build a new boat, that we were never going to make an impact if we couldn't get off the dock."

She was right. It's only by sailing on the Piscataqua River that you begin to understand its pivotal role, along with its six tributaries, in shaping the region. The Salmon Falls, the Cochecho, Bellamy, Oyster, Lamprey and Squamscott Rivers all flow into the Piscataqua, which in turn flows into the Atlantic Ocean. These waters helped to connect and grow cities and towns like Dover, Durham, Newmarket, Exeter, Newington, Portsmouth and New Castle. From the river, you can sense the close connection between the land and the water and understand that economic growth in the entire region was driven by this simple workhorse of a boat, invented by farmers.

Bolster says, "When you sail with the Gundalow Company, it's not a narrated harbor cruise. Everyone can help set the sail, haul lines or steer the boat." School children test water salinity, haul a plankton net, examine plankton under scopes and learn the basics of navigation. They see a 3-D model of the Piscataqua watershed and begin to understand the human impact on the water and the land. Adults who take part in a public or private sail get their questions answered by knowledgeable deckhands. They might learn about the history of the gundalow, the Portsmouth Naval Shipyard or an oyster reef restoration project, for example.

It's easy to think that because it was spared from an oil refinery decades ago, Great Bay (which encompasses the Piscataqua and all its tributaries) is healthy and thriving today. But so much of what we do—from building roads and sewage treatment plants to paying too little attention to our salt marshes—continues to threaten the health of the estuary. Protecting the water quality here is complicated, but on a simple level we can all understand how polluted runoff from paved areas has contributed to a decline in oysters, clams and eelgrass.

By the time the *Piscataqua* returns to the dock, Bolster hopes passengers of all ages are better informed and eager to learn more. What lives in the estuary? What is the human impact on the watershed? What can we do to become stewards of our waterways?

"If you don't first connect with a place," says Bolster, "then you will not be inclined to ask 'What can I do to protect it and make it better?'"

Selected Bibliography

Adamowicz, Joe. *The New Hiking the Monadnock Region: 44 Nature Walks and Day Hikes in the Heart of New England.* Lebanon, NH: University Press of New England, 2007.

Adler, Lisa, and Jonathan Kusel, eds. *Forest Communities, Community Forests.* Lanham, MD: Rowman & Littlefield Publisher, Inc., 2003.

Beacon, Francis B. *The Story of Lake Massabesic.* Manchester, NH: John B. Clarke, 1904.

Benner, D. "The People of the Merrimack Valley." *Merrimack Valley Magazine,* May 31, 2010.

Bennett, Jenny. "Piscataqua, a New Gundalow for New Hampshire." *Wooden Boat Magazine,* March 30, 2014.

Berger, John J. *Restoring the Earth: How Americans Are Working to Renew Our Damaged Environment.* New York: Knopf, 1987.

Burk, John S. *The Wildlife of New England.* New Hampshire: University of New Hampshire Press, 2011.

Cambridge Tribune. "For Sultry Days: The Fresh Pond Ice Company and Its Plant." April 2, 1892.

Cenkl, Pavel, ed. *Nature and Culture in the Northern Forest: Region, Heritage, and Environment in the Rural Northeast.* Iowa City: University of Iowa Press, 2010.

Chambers, Betty. *Lake Massabesic: Then and Now.* Manchester, NH: Auburn Historical Association, the Educational Continuum of Southern New Hampshire University, Audubon Center and the Manchester Historic Association, n.d.

Chestny, Linda. *Bicycling Southern New Hampshire*. Hanover, NH: University Press of New England, 2004.

Dincauze, Dena Ferran. *The Neville Site: 8,000 Years at Amoskeag*. Cambridge, MA: President and Fellows of Harvard College, 1976.

Grossi, Patricia. *The 1938 Great New England Hurricane: Looking to the Past to Understand Today's Risk*. Newark, CA: Risk Management Solutions, Inc., 2008.

Hayes, John, and Alex Wilson. *Quiet Water New Hampshire and Vermont*. 2nd ed. Boston: Appalachian Mountain Club Books, 2001.

Mansfield, Howard, ed. *Where the Mountain Stands Alone*. Lebanon, NH: University Press of New England, 2006.

Meader, J.W. *The Merrimack River: Its Sources and Tributaries*. Boston: B.B. Russell, 1869.

Parker, Edward E. *History of Brookline, Formerly Raby*. Brookline, MA: Town of Brookline, 1914.

Piscataqua Region Estuaries Partnership. *State of Our Estuaries, 2013*. University of New Hampshire, http://prepestuaries.org/science-research/past%20 SOOE-reports.

Quintal, George, Jr. *Patriots of Color: A Peculiar Beauty and Merit*. Boston: Boston National Historical Park, 2004.

Rimkunas, Barbara. "Jude Hall and His Family's Struggle." SeacoastOnline, February 28, 2014. http://www.seacoastonline.com/articles/20140228-NEWS-402280369.

Save Our Shores (SOS) Olympic Oil Refinery Scrapbook (unprocessed newsclippings, letters and flyers from various sources). Summary accessed from Milne Special Collections, University of New Hampshire Library, Durham, NH.

Smith, Sarah Shea. *They Sawed Up a Storm: The Women's Sawmill at Turkey Pond*. Portsmouth, NH: Jetty House, 1942.

Starbuck, David R. *The Archeology of New Hampshire: Exploring 10,000 Years in the Granite State*. Durham, NH: University Press of New Hampshire, 2006.

Tucker, Ian. *A Guide to 13 Trails with Nature Notes*. New Boston, NH: Piscataquog Watershed Association, 2007.

Whitney, Quincy D. *Hidden History of New Hampshire*. Charleston, SC: The History Press, 2008.

Winslow, Richard E., III. *The Piscataqua Gundalow: Workhorse for a Tidal Basin Empire*. Portsmouth, NH: Peter Randall Publisher, 1983.

Woodville (MS) Republican. "Reveal Decline of Studebaker Wealth: Depression Wipes Out Once Big Fortune." January 13, 1934.

Worcester, Samuel T. *History of the Town of Hollis, from Its First Settlement to the Year 1879*. Boston: A. Williams & Co, 1879.

Yates, Elizabeth. *Amos Fortune: Free Man*. New York: Puffin Books, 1989.

Websites

cathedralofthepines.org

des.nh.gov, New Hampshire coastal access map

dovernh.org/historic-tours

exeternh.gov/community/historic-exeter

greatbay.org

historicnewengland.org

http://www.wdl.org/en/item/2716/view/1/1 (Dunlap broadside, World Digital Library)

jaffreyhistory.org

loon.org

nhaudubon.org

nhstateparks.com/fortconstitution

poetryfoundation.org, Audio of "Poetry off the Shelf," with Robert Frost, critic Kay Ryan, September 19, 2007.

robertfrostfarm.org

seacoastnh.com/history

wildlife.state.nh.us

Index

About the Author

*L*ucie Bryar wants to encourage people to get out of their cars and into the outdoors, no matter their fitness level or experience. She started kayaking and biking about seven years ago and admits to having no special outdoor expertise or athletic skills, just a love of nature and its ability "to wash your spirit clean," in the words of Sierra Club founder John Muir.

Lucie has worked for nearly thirty years as a marketing and feature writer in banking, higher education and healthcare and has published a number of short nonfiction articles. She was at one time a featured blogger on nh.com and at paddling.net; this is her first book. She currently works for a small nonprofit serving people in need of housing and other assistance. Follow her past and future explorations around the Granite State at:

nhloveitorleafit.blogspot.com

Twitter.com/ExploreNH

Facebook.com/exploresouthernnh